Enough Is Enough

I've Been Through It All!

Author:

Elder LaTarsha M. Crenshaw

Praise of Deliverance Ministries, Inc.

Enough Is Enough: I've Been Through It All!

A true story about a battered, abused, and lost little girl who found herself before it was too late

Forward

Meeting someone is not by chance, coincidence or a stroke of luck. All of life's encounters are ordained by God! (Romans 2:10).

I was in a revival in the summer of 2007, preaching a sermon entitled, "Cheaters & Spiritual Adulterers." There I was, the young, college educated, vivacious pastor of eighteen years, broken, abused and spiritually tormented by the hurt and stain caused by past relationships and the struggle of keeping my composure while preaching to auditoriums filled with hundreds of people needing deliverance from the very same things that tormented me! I was beyond a relationship and only concerned with the mere fact of trying to get by with just my four kids, "My Jesus," and me!

Along came this beautiful young woman, dressed from head to toe with two, clean, well-dressed little girls that caught my attention. I had to admit, at first glance, that thing called love at first sight struck me. Oh yeah, it's possible especially when you're seeking God for the things that complete you and are not specific; not to mention, God has his perfect timing set for your life. It's called Destiny.

I was immediately impressed with her desire to serve God to the fullest, the southern accent, and down home hospitality better interpreted as "good cookin'." It didn't help that she would soon share the same emotions toward me. I had no idea what I was in for!

As time went on, I learned that she had more baggage then Atlanta's Hartsfield International airport. I was upset because I thought that I would get into a relationship that required minimal coaching, less spiritual struggle and everything would just be gravy. So much for that thought.

I would later learn that behind the beauty and the cover-up of the well-dressing was a lost little girl that had been through it all! I thought I was prepared to deal with anything ministry had to offer since I had gone through plenty of struggles myself and I had used them all as building points of success for the cause of educating others. Well, the pain from being raped by an uncle, his sons, and another cousin who lived in the same house, and being beaten by a guy who promised the sun, moon and stars was so deep I ended up spending more time in prayer than in love.

I learned after a brief time in the relationship how it's amazing that God is not so much as concerned with the harvest of souls, but makes specific mention of the number of laborers to gather the harvest. God knew that the harvest of souls of mankind would be plentiful and would be ready at the time of harvest. He has confidence that the seed of His word--that whenever it would fall on fertile, receptive ground, it would take root, sprout, and grow until the time of harvest. I quickly re-educated my thought process and began to focus on the five most important things that would complete the woman I needed to fulfill the thing that was lacking in our ministry. It was my purpose.

You will learn that the best builder, male or female, builds the things that will outlast them! These are five foundations you will find in this story:

A woman of strength and power – a Queen ,

A woman of wisdom and faith – a Mentor,

A woman with vision and patience – a Teacher,

A woman of integrity and experience – a Leader,

A woman of love and forgiveness – a victorious Warrior.

You must know that Elder Crenshaw is well capable of telling her life's story; after all, it did happen to her. She is an accomplished minister, writer, and the Senior Executive Officer of my ministry. She is also my wife and the mother of our seven, beautiful children. I am honored to have the pleasure of writing this forward because now have been married to her for over five years, and I have watched her grow to the place of explosion in God and I see the determination to beat the devil running.

In this book, you will be allowed to take a trip through the halls of hurt, abuse, pain, and anguish that developed the woman I am proud to call my "Elect Lady." You will find out that there is hope beyond the pain, and Joy beyond the sorrow if you find your place in God. I need to caution you. You will cry. You will get upset. You will find a loved one's experience in the hallowed pages of this true story. I did. But, in the end, you will be empowered to minister and help others bring their purpose and their destiny together to become laborers that God can use to gather the Harvest.

The desire is for readers to share the experience with others and help women who have been plagued and haunted by the pain of their past to reach the point where they too can say,

"Enough Is Enough!"

Only the best for you Baby.

Your Servant, Shepherd, & Husband,

Bishop J. C. Crenshaw II

Senior Presiding Bishop/CEO Exodus Ministries International

Published & Distributed by

Simply Elegant Publishing, LLC

To request Elder LaTarsha M. Crenshaw for book signings, speaking engagements or any other special event please contact:

praiseofdeliverance@gmail.com

ISBN: 978-0615580166

Printed in the United States of America

Table of Contents

Preface

This book is for women all over the world who have been beaten or raped, or abused physically or emotionally. I just want to let you know that you are not alone. I have been through it all but somewhere in life we have to tell ourselves, "Enough Is Enough!" When you have taken all that you can take and make up your mind that this is it, then you can give it to God. There will be people that will relate to you and there will be people that will judge you. That's ok. They judged Jesus! Just know who and what you are regardless of what you have been through. It's Never Too Late For God. If you just believe and have faith, you too will see that nothing catches God off guard. He may not be there when you expect Him to be, but He has a way of showing up right when you need Him most.

To all my ladies that read this book, I hope and pray that it will help to inspire and move you forward in life because it's time to have a made up mind.

Enough Is Enough: I've Been Through It All!

praiseofdeliverance@yolasite.com to purchase products, find information or upcoming events.

From the Author:

First, I give honor to the Lord who is the divine head of my life. Without him, I am nothing. Through it all, he saw the best in me! When I felt like giving up, He was right there. When I felt alone, He held my hand. To my parents, thank you for all you've done for me. We might not have seen eye to eye, but in the end, you were there and I love both of you. To all seven of my children, I thank you for understanding the long days and the long nights. Your understanding has helped me, and mommy loves you all. To my handsome, anointed, and talented husband, I thank you so much for being that friend, that Pastor, that Ear, that Shoulder to cry on, and last but not least, the Loving Husband and father that provides for us. I love you. Finally, to every Apostle, Bishop, Pastor, Saint, friend and family member that supported me and to every enemy that hated me, you all made life's Journey what is has been. I extend my love, gratitude, and blessing to you. Perhaps you sent a card, gave a donation, or said some encouraging words. Whatever capacity in which you rendered service, my prayer is that the God of Salvation will richly bless you and yours!

With Love,
Elder LaTarsha M. Crenshaw
Praise of Deliverance Ministries, Inc.

Chapter 1
The Birth

In the summer of 1980 Victoria A. Godwin moved to Gainesville, a small city in central Florida, with her uncle Mack and aunt Janet. Here she began her life as a young adult. Victoria began working, partying and living the fancy-free, high life. One night, she put on her best dress and the highest of high heels, did her hair and make-up and decided to go out at a local night club, have a few drinks and hang out with friends and family. As she settled in, the music was right and the taste of her strawberry daiquiri was sweet. As she sat there moving from side to side, jamming to the beat of her favorite song, and sipping on her drink she caught eyes with a man clear across the room. She would soon find out, Stony King saw her and wanted to get to know her. Stony began to walk across the room in her direction with a look that captivated her. She was excited and began to inquire of her friends. Who is that guy? What does he do for a living? Is he married? Victoria quickly learned his name and his occupation. They explained to her that Stony was an "old cat" with ten kids. She was enticed by their comments and began to look at him even the more. As he drew closer to the table, with his slick appeal, he uttered the words that would begin my story. Stony smiled and said, "Hello ladies. How are you all tonight?" Everyone responded in unison saying, "Fine." Victoria didn't say a word. Stony redirected his question to her saying, "Hmm and how are you sweet thang?" She gave a simple, sexy reply and said, "I'm fine and you?" Stony smiled and said, "I'm doing just fine now that I've seen you!" She returned the smile and asked him to have a seat. After they had exchanged pleasantries, he asked "what she was drinking?". She replied with a hint of "sex appeal", It's" that it was just a strawberry daiquiri." As the night went on, they talked, laughed, and danced. They ended the night by exchanging of phone numbers, kissing softly on the lips, and Stony telling her to sleep tight. When she got home, she told her Uncle Mack and Aunt Janet about the evening and the man she had met. She got a strange look from her Aunt Janet and a stern response from her Uncle Mack as he said, "I need to meet him because he sounds like an 'old cat.'" Victoria started laughing as her Aunt Janet looked at her and waited for her husband to leave the room so they could have "girl talk."

After a brief time, Victoria and Stony fell in love and moved in together as a couple. They played house and acted like a married couple. She was not aware of Stony's past or his secrets until he began to cheat on her with another woman. He began to treat her like trash as he had gotten what he wanted, a trophy! Victoria began to get sick and didn't know what was wrong with her so she made a doctor appointment at the local hospital. As she was feeling alone and scared, and thinking the worst, the doctor knocked on the door. As Victoria looked up with tears in her eyes, the doctor looked at her and said, "Congratulations, you are pregnant!" She began to cry and screamed, "No, I can't be!" The doctor repeatedly informed that she was four weeks pregnant. Briefly, she stopped crying and talked with the doctor about the pregnancy do's and the don'ts of pregnancy. This would be the beginning of the journey of my life.

Victoria informed her family members that told she was with child. After mustering up strength, she called her mother, Mrs. Mae Mae Godwin, who lived in Mobile,

Alabama for guidance. Mae Mae also told her about the pregnancy do's and the don'ts. Victoria told her mother she was fine and everything would work out. Mae Mae laughed and said, "Okay miss hot ass!" After talking with Mae Mae, she decided to talk with Stony later that night when he got home, as moving back to her hometown was not an option. Stony arrived home from work as always hugging and kissing Victoria. He looked at her and said, "What's wrong? Why you looking like that?" She looked at him in the face and said, "Well, you're about to be a father for the eleventh time!" Stony was happy when he heard the news.

Time went on and Victoria continued working and playing housewife. As she neared the end of her pregnancy, she found out Stony was cheating on her and had another woman pregnant!

On January 8, 1983 at the local hospital, Victoria and Stony welcomed a six-pound baby girl, Kashia LaDonna King, yelling at the top of her lungs. She was tiny, very light-skinned with brown freckles on her face, and had a head full of hair. That was the happiest day of her mother's life. After the doctors came back in the room to take the new baby for testing, Victoria and Stony got into an argument because Stony was leaving the hospital to go home. Little did she know he was going to be with another woman.

After a brief stay in the hospital, Victoria and her baby girl were able to go home. Stony didn't even go get them; instead, he made a bad decision and sent his niece. The niece, Kelly, is so inclined to share some of the reasons why Stony wasn't as involved while she was in the hospital. She began to tell Victoria all the things that Stony was doing. Kelly told Victoria that Stony was laying up with this woman named Lisa. The more she told Victoria, the more Victoria gets upset. Later that night when Stony got home, she asked him where he had been. Stony lied and told her he was over his sister's house. Victoria said stop lying you've been out with Lisa! They began to argue and fight. The yelling and fighting continued the entire week.

Baby Kashia started getting sick and was in and out of the hospital. The doctors didn't know what was wrong with the infant as her hands and feet would get real sweaty and then turn ice cold as though she were dead! Young Victoria was in a lonely place;; she was scared as she didn't know what to do. Sleep deprived, concerned, and confused, as matters were not getting any better at home, Victoria called her mother. Her mother insisted that they come home, but Victoria didn't want to go back to Mobile, Alabama as she had a good job, friends, a nice house, a new baby, and a piece of a man. To her, she was doing it big!

One day Victoria decided she had enough of Stony. She was going to look for him and see if he was at his sister's house as he had so frequently claimed. She got in her car and went to the sister's house. And, to her surprise, there he was sitting in the living room with "the other woman," Lisa. Victoria began to snap by cursing and yelling at him and the woman. Stony jumped up yelling, hitting, and cursing her as numerous family members looked on and did nothing. Victoria went back home and called her mother Mae Mae, her sister Deidre, and all five of her brothers:, Mike, Earl, KG, George, and Robert. They began to prepare to come to Mobile that weekend.

It was pouring down rain that night when Stony returned home. He began hitting and cursing Victoria. As she tried to fight back, he stopped, then looked at her, and told her to get the baby and get out of his house! All of a sudden, Victoria and her infant are in the rain, in the dead of night and, alone, with no car, no money, no nothing. She went to a friend's house for the night and later called her mother and told her what happened. Mae Mae was hot! Angry, concerned, and wanting assurance that she had somewhere to stay for the night, Mae Mae committed to send her some money the next day. While Victoria sat there on the phone crying and talking to her mother, she and realized there was a strong possibility that she couldn't live, work, and raise an infant by herself. Mae Mae came to get the two-week old infant Kashia for what was supposed to be a brief while until Victoria could get back on her feet.

Chapter 2
At Grandma's House

Well here I am, Kashia. Since I was a few months old, I've been living with my granny, Ms. Godwin, in Mobile, in the big green house with my aunt Deidre and her two boys, and my uncles, Keno and DeWayne. I was in heaven. I was the baby girl of the house and all eyes were on me. I was really the only girl in the house. My aunt, although she was with her kids' father, was really into women and would act like one of the guys. So, I was the only girl in the house most of the time when my granny, who worked, wasn't there. I was in the hands of my uncles and aunt. But, that was ok because I got anything I wanted. Kashia got to stay up as late as she wanted. Once again, I felt like I was in heaven. My uncles and aunt were known as big time drug dealers in Mobile. They had a lot of money, many cars, many ladies, the finest clothes, and a lot of gold on their hands, around their neck, and in their mouth. And because I was the new kid on the block I got to wear name brand clothes, name brand shoes, and gold around my neck. I also got to go where my uncles went. All of the women loved me. I got to stay at their house, eat what I wanted to eat, and play with whatever I wanted to play with. I was learning how to live the good life. Even through all of that, I still missed my mommy and I wanted to go back home and be with my mommy. My mother would call every day and ask me what I was doing, and every day I would tell her that I was having fun with my uncles and my cousins. She would laugh and yes that good mommy will be down there soon to get you. I would get happy and say ok mom I gotta go my Uncle Jack is leaving me. After I would get off the phone with my mother, my uncle would see that I was sad because my mother wasn't there and I was too young to know what was going on. To make me feel better he would take me around the corner to Red Dot, the hood store where all the gum was one cent. I liked that store and I got a big bag of one cent gum. Everybody knew my folks; I got what I wanted from the men and the women. I learned that lifestyle fast. My uncle taught me how to get what I wanted, when I wanted it. He would go up to a woman and tell me to tell her to give me some money. If she didn't give it to me, I was to curse her out, kick her or hit her to make her give me the money. If anyone said anything to me wrong my uncles were going to hurt them. When people, women and men, would see me around the corner with my folks, they knew they had to give me something or buy me something. I felt like I was a princess. You could tell me nothing because if you said anything wrong to me I was going to get my uncles and my auntie because they were the Jones' and everybody knew not to mess with the Godwin's. As I got up in age I started to notice that what my family was doing was wrong. Every other month my granny's door would get kicked in by the police. My cousin, my granny, and I would be sitting in the den looking at TV when I would see the red and blue lights. I would hop up and say granny lights lights outside. And, before she could get up the police were knocking down our door. I would start crying; my cousin would start crying; and granny would be yelling at the police. The police had all of us sit in the den as they would go throw the house pulling the clothes out of the drawers and throwing them on the floor. The police would take everything out the closet and throw it on the floor. They would go through my granny's refrigerator and take out the food. Then, the police would go out to her cars to see if they could find drugs. After they left my granny would call my uncles and my aunt to let them know that the police just left her house looking for drugs. My uncles and aunt would not come home that night. It was crazy because in the next few weeks my uncles would know who told on them. They would always bring that person back to my granny house and they would make me and my cousin go in the back room until they got done talking. Only they weren't really talking, they were beating that person real bad.

It was at that time I didn't want to stay there anymore. Because the police were coming to our house and being mean to us, my uncles were being mean to people. I would cry every night and say mommy why won't you come and get me. When she called, I couldn't tell her what happened because I was scared I was going to get in trouble or get beat like they beat the people who told on them. So heaven now felt like hell. My granny was getting mad at everybody in the house. She wanted everybody to get out. There was no more living the good life. I went from wearing name brands from the mall to wearing Mark-K and Sale-Mart clothes. There was no more staying the night with my uncles' girlfriends. No more nothing, granny had shut it down. She started yelling a lot, and cursing a lot. She stopped calling me her baby and asking me to come here little this and little that. It was Hell; I didn't want to be there I was sitting there mad at my mother because she sent me here with this people. I thought to myself: What did I do to be here? Did my mother not want me because of what my dad did? Was I supposed to be here on earth? I didn't know. But what I did know was I was ready to go back home with my mother and my father. I wanted things to be right again like I thought it was supposed to be, my dad, my mom, and me. But it didn't happen. As if things couldn't get any worse, my father tried calling me at my granny house. I wasn't allow to talk to him and he couldn't come see me because if he would have my uncles were going to jump on him because he hit my mother and put us out in the rain. Now I'm really sitting there because I want my dad and no one would let me see him or talk to him.

As the months went on, things didn't change. The police were still kicking in my granny's door and looking for drugs. Sometimes they found them. My uncles started going to jail one by one. Sometimes one uncle would be getting out and the other uncle would be going in. Then, my aunt started going to jail. So now all that's left are an uncle, my two cousins, DeWayne and Keon, and me at home with granny. Now I'm alone no one here but us. I would cry night after night because I was ready to go home with my mother. I'm also ready to see my dad. The last time I saw him, I was just two weeks old. I really don't know much about my dad but bad things, because all my granny and my mother tell me are bad things about him like how he put us out when I two weeks old, that he don't love me and if he did he wouldn't have put us out. They tell me he loves his other kids more than he loves me. So all I knew as a child, was that my father was no good, he put us out when I was two weeks old, he had a lot of kids, he painted cars, and he was not going to send me any money because he didn't love me. I believed all of that until I was about four.

One Christmas Stony mailed me a box. And in that box, was a box of cookies and a guitar. Out of every gift I had, that was my best gift because my daddy sent it. All those years my granny and mother told me my daddy didn't love me, I now knew it wasn't true. So as I sat there playing the guitar and singing with my box of cookies on my lap, my grandmother says that all he sent you that ain't 'bout (s***). And at that moment my Christmas was ruined. Once again I had to hear my grandmother talk about my dad. If that wasn't enough, my mom called to see what my dad bought, not to say Merry Christmas or I love you, but to see what my dad had got me. And as I told her she laughed and said you can throw that (s***) in the trash. So as I handed the phone to my granny, she told my granny to throw my cookies and guitar in the trash. So once again I'm mad and hating my mother and my granny. If that wasn't enough, she called to tell us about this new man that she had been dating for about two in half years and that he asked her to marry him. So even with me being mad I was happy because this now means I get to go back home with my mom and I will get a new dad and see my real dad. (Smile) That day my mom and granny talk about me going back home to live with her. My grandmother asked me if I wanted to go live with my mother. Just that fast I forgot I hated her and I jumped up and down saying yes I do.

After granny told my mother I said yes, my mother put her husband to be and my soon to be dad, Von, on the phone and let me talk to him. We talked for about ten minutes; he was talking what I wanted to hear. He let me know that I was coming back home with him and my mother and he was going to be a daddy. I was filled with joy to know that I was going home with my mom and my new dad, and that I was going to be in another big house with my own room. I was also getting to dress up in a big dress with flowers at my mother's wedding. I was leaving hell and getting ready to back to heaven, or so I thought.

Chapter 3
Life with Momma

Welcome home! Home sweet home. I'm home with my mother and soon to be new daddy. Great. It was my first day home with my mother and my father to be. As my mom gets out the car to unlock the door to the house, my heart is overjoyed because I have left hell and I'm on my way to enter heaven again. As my mom and I walk through the house she shows me the big den, the big living room, and the big kitchen. She shows me her and my new dad's bedroom with the big bathroom. Wow, I thought to myself, my mom and new dad are rich just like my uncles and auntie. I thought about what my folks in Mobile did to have all that nice stuff. Then my mom showed me my room. I had a big room too just without the bathroom. I had two beds in my room with a big dresser and a lot of clothes and shoes and a lot of toys that were all mine. I was very happy. I turned around and my mom was standing there smiling. Then she asked me if I liked my room. I remember smiling, giving her a big hug, telling her I loved her and waiting for her to tell me she loved me. But she didn't. All she said was hmm, this is your room and these are your toys and your clothes. You've got to keep your room clean. If you don't you will get a whipping. I replied with a yes ma'am. Then my new soon to be daddy came in my room and asked if I liked my room. I looked at him, gave him a hug, told him thank you and said I love you. He replied that he loved me too. As I looked at him and said to myself, he loves me back, that's when I put my trust in him. We began to be the best of friends. He was my dad and I didn't see any wrong in him. When I would do wrong and I knew I was going to get in trouble, he would keep me from getting a whipping. He would buy me what I wanted—it was all about little old me. I could do no wrong. All he saw was a good little girl that was sweet. He couldn't see why would a man put his woman and child out. Never once did he talk bad of my dad. He would say good things about my dad, so I'm loving him even more because he was the only one that didn't talk bad about my dad, at least not while I was around. Months and months went by and everything was good. I was in heaven; I had it all. As me and Von got closer, I could see that something was wrong with my mother but I didn't know what because I was too young to understand. My mother was getting upset because it was more about me and not her, at least that is what I thought. Time went on and as we got closer to that big day I was really happy because Von was getting ready to be my daddy and our family would be complete. As I go with my mom to pick out my dress and my shoes, I looked at my mother and said I wanted to be in the wedding. She said I was her flower girl. I was overjoyed to know I would be dressed up as a pretty flower girl in my big ivory dress with the white flowers on it, my ivory shiny shoes with flowers on them, and pretty flowers in my long jerry curly hair. I couldn't wait to dress up and look like a princess. So, as they came me, and my mother, her friends, and her sister and brothers were getting dressed for the wedding. My mother was so scared. I was laughing. My family was back in the room with us laughing and making jokes about my mom. As she smiled I saw her happy as if it were the day she had me. I sat there watching my mother get dressed for her big day. She really looked happy, as she put on her a pretty white slip and did her hair and make-up. Then she stood up so that her mother could dress her in her ivory beaded dress with the long train. As my granny zipped her up from the back I saw my grandmother with water in her eyes. I didn't know why she was crying, so I asked her. She looked at me and said that one day when I have a child and my child gets married, I would understand. Still not understanding but knowing she wasn't sad, but that she was happy for my mother and so was I, I started crying also. But my cry was a loud cry because I didn't know how to cry quiet. So the wedding is here my mother and my new dad are one; now we are a whole family. Now it's time for their honeymoon and that means I've got to go stay with granny for a week. I don't want to go. That place is hell. I cried I acted up because I didn't want to go. But once my step dad talked to me and brought me a new doll, I was fine and I said ok I will go. So as my parents got ready to leave on their honeymoon, I sat at the door crying as that red '86 Lincoln town car left.

Ok, back to Mobile for a week, I was a real brat. I didn't want to listen. I was cursing and telling people what I was and what I wasn't going to do because that's what I knew to do while I was there because that's what I was taught by my uncles. But what they failed to tell me was that only works around the corner with the folks around the corner. I found out quickly as granny gave me my first whipping. I thought she was the devil because she hit me and I don't get hit by no one unless it's my mommy. I was really ready to go back home. As I went upstairs and sat in the middle of the floor in the room, I began to yell and curse as if I were grown. My uncles and my auntie just laughed as if I were a show or something. My grandmother went outside and got switches and put them together and came up stairs and pulled my drawers down and whipped me until I had marks all over my butt. Oh my god. I really thought she was the devil. I hated her; I wanted to go home and never come back. That's when I found out you don't talk to granny or any grown person like that. The week went by and my mom and my stepdad came back. Boy was I happy because my daddy was here and nobody could hit me or be mean to me while he was around.

So as they're back, my mother asked my granny how was everything. Granny said well I had to whip your child 'cause she cursed me and told me what she was and wasn't going to do. My mother laughed asked my granny why was I still alive. My stepfather did think that was funny and he was taking up for me and said, well who taught her that, she had to hear it from one of you all. So my granny and my stepdad got into it as I sat again crying and wanting to go home. But we still had to stay for two more days before we went home. As that morning comes, we pack up the car to leave. Yes! Ready to get back to my room, back to heaven.

As time went on things were good. I had my mother and my stepdad. I wasn't really worried about my real dad because I had Von and I got what I wanted physically and emotionally. As everything was going good, one night I was in my room and I heard my mom and my stepdad yelling and I didn't know what was going on. I got up and walked in the kitchen and I saw my stepdad hitting my mother. I began crying and saying stop don't hit my mommy. My mom looked up and told me to go in my room. I told her no and that's when my stepdad yelled at me and told me to get of there and go in my room. It was then that I became mad at him. I hated him because he was hitting my mom and because he yelled at me. Although it went on for minutes, it felt like hours. As I sat there in my room crying, wanting my real dad, hating my stepdad, I wanted to hit him for hitting my mom. It was then I said he don't love me or my mommy because he's being mean to us and he hit my mommy. After a while I heard the door close and my mother came in my room. I looked up at her, her shirt was ripped; her nose was bleeding. Her eye was black and she was crying. I looked at her and started crying. She held me and said I'm ok, I love you. That was the first time I heard my mother tell me she loved me. So now I'm really mad at Von. I hated him. I wanted to hit him in his eye and make his nose bleed.

After everything calmed down, my stepdad came back home. My mom was scared because she didn't know what was next. But he came in and told me and my mother he was sorry and it would never happen again. That was a lie. It got worse. Every other week they were fighting and yelling. My mother would have marks on her. My stepdad would have marks on him. I was getting very angry with my stepdad. I didn't care if my mom did something or not. I was mad at him. I wanted him dead and wished my uncle would have come and killed him or beat him like they beat them people in Mobile. But no one knew what was going on because my mom didn't tell anybody but my stepdad's family and they didn't care they was on his side they really didn't like my mom from the get go.

We sat up in that house day and night waiting to see if Von was going to yell or hit my mom about something. If the food was cold, he got mad. If my room was messed up, he get mad. If shoes were on the floor in his way, he got mad. If she messed with his stuff, he got mad. We didn't know what to think when he got home. He let his oldest son, Drew come stay. Drew would see how his dad was doing my mother and Drew thought he could do it too. That's when my mother said enough is enough. I was sitting in the den with my step brother and my stepdad. My mom was in the kitchen getting ready to cook for us when Drew came in the kitchen talking to my mother in any kind of way. My mom and Drew got into it. My stepdad hopped up and went into the kitchen and he started yelling at my mom. I sat in the den crying I got up and stood in the door way and I started yelling for them to stop. But once again, they told me to go in my room. This time I didn't go because it was two against one. My mom pulled out a big knife and told Von to get out of her house or he would die that day. As I stood there crying, Drew left and didn't come back, but my stepdad was so mad at my mom he grabbed her by her clothes and hit her. She dropped the knife. She and my stepdad were fighting bad. I went into the kitchen to stop them, but they wouldn't stop, I thought my mom was going to die that day. When they stopped, my mom said this is it, I'm done. I want a divorce. I don't want to be with you no more. I can't take you beating on me and now letting your child talk to be any kind of way. It's not going to work. My stepdad walked out. I never saw him again.

My mother called my granny and told her what was going on. That day my granny and my auntie and my uncles left Mobile to come to Gainesville. I was happy 'cause I thought my uncles were coming to kill my step dad. But when my granny got to my mother's house, they talked and my mother told her to take me back with her until after the divorce and she got back on her feet. So I leave my mother again to go stay with my grandmother. This time I would be there for about a year or two.

Back with my granny ,things were still the same--police kicking in the door, my family in and out of jail, yelling and fighting going on in the house. Oh well, I had to deal with it. I'm here and this where I would be until my mommy comes and gets me. I was in pre-kindergarten. Here, I met a little boy by the name of Mario. He was the same age as me. He was mixed; his mother was white and his dad was black. Every day he would sit by me and give me his snack at play time. He would always want to play house. He wanted me to be his wife, so I would be mommy and he was daddy. One day Mario came to school with his mother's wedding ring. They had money; his mother's ring was about 24 or 36 karat gold. Mario brought the ring to school and gave it to me while we were at play time and said, "I want you to be my wife." I showed my teacher and the teacher laughed. I thought I was in love. Everyone told me they loved, but now this little boy has given me a ring. I thought he loved me.

The teacher called Mario's parents and my granny and my aunt to come to the school. When our parents got to the school, the teacher told my granny and Mario's mother what he did. His mom was so mad she said, "I was looking for my ring. I thought I had lost it." They my aunt asked Mario, "What was you thinking?" Mario said, "I was thinking she was going to my wife. I love her lips, that's why I wanted to marry her." The teacher and our parents started laughing. Later, Mario's mother brought him a little fake ring to give to me and we said we were going to get married. After the end of kindergarten, I never saw Mario again.

Chapter 4
The runaway minor

Time went on and I still stayed with granny going to school me and my cousins it was at this time Mike came back home from the army. Once again I was the only girl in the house. I did everything my cousins did. Me and my cousin Cedi got into everything; we were really bad. I knew my mom wasn't coming back for me for a long time, so I fit in where I was at. My cousin and I were in school together; I was in the second grade and he was in the third grade. This is when I learned my Uncle Mike was really mean and crazy. He was the uncle who used to say, "This is my niece, my baby, uncle's little girl." But this day my cousin and I got in trouble at school and the school called my granny. When we got home my granny said, "I'm not going to whip you, your daddy going to whip you." But since I was uncle's little girl, I didn't think it would that bad. When Uncle Mike got home, he walked in, called us downstairs, and asked us what we did. We told him what we did and why we did it. My uncle went out to his car and got a big, thick, two by four paddle made of real wood. In my mind I was thinking he was just going to scare us. But he didn't. He beat Cedi until his butt bled. Then it was my turn. He laid me across his lap and hit me over and over on my butt with that two by four wood paddle. My grandmother did nothing but cursed us out saying, " I bet your ass won't act up again!" It was at that time that I was ready to go home because every time we got into trouble my uncle whipped us. I hated him because he didn't have to beat us like that. They never let me talk to my mother after I got a whipping because they knew I would tell my mom and my granny had this saying, what happen in my house, stay in my house.

When I did talk to my mom, I told her I wanted to come home. She asked me what was wrong and I told her my uncle was whipping me with a paddle made out of wood and it was leaving big marks on my butt. So she got mad and asked my granny what was my uncle doing hitting me. So my mom and my granny argued. When my mom and grandmother got off the phone, my granny went off on me and I got another whipping from my granny. My aunt was mad and she started arguing with my granny. The next thing knew, I was in the wrong.

Summer was almost here and school was about to be out. I knew I only had a month left there at granny's house, thank God. I thought I would be out of hell for real this time because I wouldn't be there with my grandmother. My mom and my stepdad were not together, so it would just be me and my mommy, which was great. It would be just us with no one else in the way. My mommy could have me all to herself and could have my mommy all to myself.

As the summer came and the last day of school was here, I went home that day and I began looking around the house and saying to myself, "Bye, bye hell, I won't be back. I won't be getting beat from that man no more and I don't have to be sad no more. I will be home with my mommy where my mommy loves me and won't hit me." Little did I know that my life was going to get worse!

I returned home to Mobile. My mom had moved into a new apartment. The apartment had a nice sized backyard and a little front yard. I couldn't play in the front yard because it was too close to the highway. The apartment wasn't like our old house, but it was nice. I didn't care. I was just happy to be back home with my mother. I didn't have to be beat or cursed out or live the life as I did in Mobile. I knew my mom wouldn't let anything happen to me. I didn't know anyone there but my family and one or two of my mother friends because I had been gone so long. My mother's friend, Mrs. Ross, had kids that were way older than me except her last child, Chantey. Chantey and I were two years apart and our birthdays were on the same day. Chantey was also my mother's godchild. At first I didn't like Chantey because she had spent more time with my mother than I did. But, after a while we began to be best friends. We stayed over each other's house; we went to school together; we had our birthday party together; we did everything together. When you saw me, you saw her and when you saw her, you saw me. Over the summer, I noticed something about my mother that just wasn't right. She didn't act the way she used to when I was a little girl. She was mean and she didn't like to do anything with me. She would work, come home, look at TV, and go out on weekends with her friends. I would have to stay over Chantey's house all weekend. So even though I had a friend, I was sad because my mom wasn't there like I thought she would be. Yes, she brought me new clothes, did my hair so pretty, and I had all the toys I could want my own room, but what I was missing was her. So I began to ask her when I would see her getting ready for the weekend, where are you going? She wouldn't lie to me. She would always say I'm going to find you a new daddy. Then I would ask her if that meant I had to go to Chantey's house again. And she would say yes. I would get upset and she would yell at me. Her voice alone made me cry and get scared because I knew that something would happen while I was gone. She wasn't the sweet talking mommy I knew. She would yell and say I've got to find you a daddy because your (d***) daddy ain't here and he ain't trying to do nothing for you. So here again I got to hear her talk about my dad again. So I would get mad and I started disliking mom I began to hate her. I did want to be around her. I wanted to stay with my real dad. I felt like my mother didn't love me because what my dad had done to her and because I looked more like my dad. When she saw me, she saw my dad. I just knew I hated her and the way she was doing me, but I said oh well, as long as she's not beating me with big stick. So as the summer came to an end, my mother got me ready for school. Third grade here I come. Little did I know that my dad's cousin was working at the school. She knew who I was because she had seen me at church with my mother. So here I am on the first day of school with new clothes, new shoes, new hairdo, and new book bag. I was ready for school looked like I belong to the rich and famous, but on the inside I was sad and mad and ready to hurt my mother. And I knew just how I was going to do it. Time will surely tell, how as a seven-year old I had the mind of a sixteen-year old. On the first day of school everything was good. I went to lunch and saw my dad cousin's Val. As I walked through the lunch line, cousin Val was standing there waiting to give me a hug and a kiss. As I got closer to her she smiled and said hi baby how is you? Give me a hug. Do you know who I am? As I stood there with so much I wanted to say and ask, I said yes ma'am you are cousin Val, my daddy's cousin. She began smiling harder because I knew who she was., She asked me if I had seen my daddy. I replied saying no ma'am. But my inside was saying (but you're about to lead me to him). She said well I've got to tell him I saw you and you go to my school. I said ok. In my head I was saying you do that. So after school Chantey's mother came and picked us up after school. The deal was my mom would take me and Chantey to school and Mrs. Ross would pick us up after. My plan was working out just fine. So that day I went home I told my mother I saw my dad's cousin and that she worked in the launch room. Oh my god. Why did I tell her that? She went off on me. She was like, so what you're not going to his house and he's not coming over here. So you can get that (s****) out of your head. I don't love him and he don't love you. He ain't did nothing for you. Don't say his name in my house no more and if you can't do what I say, then you can go live with him and all his whores or you can go back to Mobile so your uncle can beat you a board, After she said that I began to cry because I didn't know what I had done that was so bad and why I couldn't be in my daddy's life. So as I went to school, day by day I was getting more info on my dad. I wanted to know where he stayed and how he looked. One day I talked to Chantey about my problems. Chantey waited until I went home to tell her mother. The next morning when we got to Chantey granny's house, Mrs. Ross, me, my mom and Chantey sat down at the table and Mrs. Ross talked to my mother about me going to see my dad. And as she was talking to my mother, my mother looked at me and as I was sitting there I knew I was going to get in trouble. So I began to get mad at Chantey because I told her not to say anything to no one. So as the days went on I saw my dad's cousin at school. She would tell me your dad says hi and she would give me ten dollars and say this is from your dad, he wants to come see you but your mom won't tell him where she stays. I was mad but I didn't say much because

I knew I was already in trouble when I got home because of what I told Chantey. So later in the day when I got home, I told my mom my dad gave me ten dollars and she said what do you mean your dad gave you ten dollars? She said he came to your school and you saw your dad. I said no he gave the money to cousin Val. She got on the phone and called my cousin Val. As she sat there on the phone with my cousin, she began to get madder and madder. Then she started going off on my cousin and calling her all kind of (b****) and (w****). Then she started talking about my dad in a very bad way. After she hung up the phone, she came in the room yelling and hitting me with her hand and calling me ungrateful and telling me I wasn't nothing and I was going to be just like my daddy. I laid there crying for her to stop. After I got up I went into the bathroom to run some water in the tub to take a bath. I looked at my face. My nose was bleeding; my lip was busted. My head was bleeding because the beads in my head had hit the wall and pushed the beads back in my head. As I looked at myself in the mirror, my mother came in the restroom where I was and yelled again at me and said that's what I get for being hard-headed and grown. I sat in the tub crying and hating my mother even more. I wished she was dead. I sat there thinking of ways to hurt her while she slept. But, the only thing I could think of was going to be with my dad and how I was going to get there. So as months went by, I acted out the more so she would take me to see my dad. The more I acted out, the more I got beat with a belt, a shoe, switch or her fist. So I would tell Chantey and she would tell her mother. The more I said to Chantey, the more she told her mother. I began to hate Chantey and her mother because they thought they were helping me, but they were really getting me beat by my mother. Mrs. Ross was very messy. She would say stuff to my mother about me just to see my mother go off on me. I really hated that lady. I didn't want her around me. I didn't want her child to be around me. So one day my mother made up in her mind she was going to let me go and meet my dad. She called him and asked him if he wanted to see me. He said yes, so one day when she got off work she took me over his house. I found out that he stayed right down the street from my school. It was a walk, but his niece Pam stayed in walking distance of my school. I went to his house that day. I was so happy and he was too. He hugged and kissed me so hard and he kept saying I love you. I told him I love you too. So as me and my father talked, my mother was getting mad saying crazy stuff out her mouth to my dad. Ladies, you know how we do. Hmm. So my dad was getting mad, but he didn't yell or anything in front of me. He reached in his pocket, pulled out some money and gave it to me. After that we got ready to leave. I looked back and blew my dad a kiss and said I love you. He looked back at me, blew me a kiss and said I love you too, honey. Time went on. I was getting a little bit better because I had seen my dad and my mother let me talk to him from time to time. Sometimes, she would let me go over his house on Saturdays and hang out with him and my little brother Jake. But one day, my mom had hell in her and asked my dad about child support. He said he wasn't working, so my mom got mad at him and stopped me from going over there again. But, I would still hear from him through his cousin at the school. I would never tell my mom because I knew if I did, I would get beat again and I was already getting whippings because of my grades in school. So to keep from adding gas to the fire, I didn't say anything. As time went on, I was still getting beat for whatever reason whether I was wrong or right.

Every day I was abused either physically or emotionally. I made up in my mind that I was going to leave my mother and hurt her like she hurt me. So, I went to school and cut up. The teacher called my mother; I knew what I was doing because we were just learning about HRS ,human rescue system, in school. If you had a mark on you, your parent could get in trouble. So that day when I got home, my mother beat me, she beat me good. I had welts on my back from her belt. She hit me in my face so my face was red as fire. My nose was bleeding and she couldn't get it to stop so I had to put ice on my nose and hold my head back. She beat me so bad it hurt to sit down. The next day my mother told me to wear long pants and a shirt so the teacher couldn't see the marks on me so when I got to school. I was so mad at my mother. I hated her and today was the day I was going to hurt her. I went to school and when I got in class I sat down at the desk and started crying. I wouldn't say anything to my teacher. My teacher said Kashia, we're going to have a good day to day. I didn't say anything. I just started crying harder. The teacher told me to come to her. When I got up, I put my hands on my butt and my teacher asked what was wrong. I said because of you I got beat. She asked what I meant. I said you called my mother and I got beat. The teacher took me in the bathroom and made me pull up my clothes. As she looked at my back and my butt, she grabbed her mouth and started crying saying what did I do. I said you told on me and that made my mommy mad, Mrs. Kent went to the office and got the nurse,. When the nurse came back in the room, she had her camera ready to take photos. They called HRS to come to the school. I was waiting for HRS to come get me, but all they did was take photos and tell me don't worry, they would get me out of my house soon, but for now, I would have to go back home with my mother. I cried because I knew I was going to die if she found out. When she came and got me, she didn't say anything. I thought, good, I'm not in trouble today. But, she didn't say anything because we were at Chantey's granny house. But when we got in the car to go home, she began to yell and ask me why did I call them folks on her. I didn't say anything so she began to yell and hit me in my face and in my head. I began to cry and say I don't know. So she said I'm going to give you something to call for. When we got home, she began hitting me over and over in my face, in my head, and in my back. Wherever she could hit me and whatever she could hit me with. My lip was busted up real bad. It was blue black. After she got done hitting me, she picked up the phone and said call the police, I dare you. I was scared. I just went in my room and started sticking my arm with a pen trying to kill myself. So the next day as I got ready for school, I looked around my room and said good bye room, good bye house, this is my last day here with you. As we got ready to pick up Brea that next day for school, my mother and Ms. Ross were talking about me and how I told them people on her. Ms. Ross looked at me and my body and said you should have been my child cause I would have killed you if would have sent those people to my job. I looked at her. In my head I was calling her all kind of nasty names and saying you don't have to worry about me neither cause this is my last day seeing you and your ugly black child looking like an ape. My mother dropped us off at school and before I got out of the car she said let them white people come to my job today and see what's going to happen to you. I replied, yes ma'am. But, I wanted to say oh they will be there cause I won't be here when you come get me today. I went all day in school looking at the clock. My teacher asked me if was

I better. I just looked at her ready to go off on her, but said nope, but I will be after today. She looked at me as if she wanted to say what do mean, but she didn't. She just looked at me. It was time for school to be out. The call for the walkers came first, then the car riders, then the after school kids and the bus riders. That was perfect because when they called for the walkers I got up and walked out to the road crosser. My teacher didn't say anything, so I kept walking.

When I got to the lady who walked the kids across the road, she said where is your note, Are you a new kid? I told her I was a new kid in school. She told me to have my mother write me a note for tomorrow. I said yes ma'am, but I knew I wouldn't be back. As she lead the kids across the road, I looked back one last time and said bye-bye. Then, I turned around and began walking. I knew I couldn't walk all the way down to my father's house because that was about ten miles. But my daddy's niece stayed about a block away from my school. I walked to my cousin's house. With every step I took, I was saying I free from that (b****). I hate you. I wish you die.

Chapter 5
Daddy's Little Girl

Knock, knock! Who is it cousin Kelly asked? Kashia, Who's Kashia? As the door opened, I stood there crying as Kelly asked, baby what's wrong? Where is your mother? I replied by saying she is at work and she doesn't know I'm here. I ran away from school. Please don't call my mother, I don't want to go back there. Please, my mother beat me and I told HRS the other day at school, but they made me go back home. They went on her job and that just made her madder and she beat me again. As cousin Kelly said baby come in the house, she then said what do you want me to do? I said I want my daddy. I want to stay with my daddy, but she won't let me see my daddy. I want my daddy. Kelly called Stony and told him I had run away from home because I was getting beat and wanted him. So my father jumped in his truck and came to Kelly's house. When he got there, he ran up to me and hugged me. I just started crying and saying I want to go with you; I don't want to go home. So he took me to his house and called HRS and told them what happened. HRS came out to my dad's house and took photos again. The HRS lady, Ms. Whitefield, said we were just at your school yesterday. I said I know, and I told you I didn't want to go back but you made me and I got beat again. My dad got mad and said why would you let her go back if she had marks on her in the first place? They didn't have anything to say. As the lady kept taking more photos, she saw there were some fresh marks that weren't there the other day. HRS wrote in my file that they told my father I could stay with him for a few days, but I would have to be placed in a foster home for a while until the court approved and my father's house was up to par.

So they left. My dad and I talked and like any young child I told him everything that my mama and any other relatives said. So we talked and we talked and he told me why he and my mother spilt. I found out that he was cheating, but a lot of it was because of my mother's family and the way my mother would talk to my dad as if he were a child or a dog. I cried. I was upset. But I was also ok with it all because I knew I wasn't going to get beat anymore. I had someone that knew what I was going through because he had lived with my mother for some years. He was just happy to have me in his life and he kept telling me he loved me and he was not going to let anyone hurt me. But I was still a little scared because I knew the police had to tell my mother where I was and I thought she was going to come get me. But she didn't. Even though I didn't want to be there with her, I wanted her to hurt like she hurt me. I still wanted her to show that she cared by coming to get me or showing up. But, she didn't. I knew from that, that she didn't love me or care about me. At least that was what I thought because I didn't know what the police had told her. A few days passed and when I didn't go to school, my teacher got worried. I didn't know my teacher, Mrs. Kent, was a foster parent. But, she went to the office at school and they told her what had happened and that I would be with my dad for a few days until they could find a home to put me in. Mrs. Kent told the school she would take me because I one of her students and she would love to have me. Since I wouldn't have to change schools, the school thought Mrs. Kent taking me was a good idea and contacted HRS to let them know. HRS came back to my dad's house that Friday and told him they had found a home for me. I started crying because I enjoyed being with my dad, but they said don't cry, you are going to stay with your teacher, Mrs. Kent and you will come see your dad on the weekends until they do the paperwork for you to come stay with your father. I looked at my father and said is that ok dad? Will I be ok? He smile and wiped the tears from my face and said yes honey, it's going to be ok. No one will hurt you. Your mother is not allowed to come near you at all. If she does, she will go to jail. I looked at the lady from HRS. She smile and said dear you're going to be fine. Mrs. Kent is very nice. She has a big three bedroom and two bathroom house with a big den and a big living room.

She has a swimming pool, a big front and back yard. It's just her and her husband living there with their two dogs. I smiled and I thought about my mother and her house when she was married to Von. We just didn't have a swimming pool. So I was happy to know I would be living with someone that was nicer.. So the lady from HRS told me to go get my stuff and tell my dad goodbye. As I got ready to leave, I went in my little brother Jay's room and I told him that I would see him later and I would be back soon to play with him. He looked at me and said, don't go I love you hurry back ok, I respond by saying I will as I went back in the living room with my dad and the lady from HRS I looked at my dad and said I love you see you soon he said ok honey I love you be good daddy will see you next weekend. As I got into the car, I looked up and blew my dad a kiss and I love you as Ms. Whitefield said you have a nice dad I will do everything in power to fix it where you will be with your dad. As we are driving to

Mrs. Kent's house, I was so scared because one, I was scared of dogs; and two, I didn't know how Mrs. And her husband were going to act because a black child was coming to live with them for a while. So here we are pulling up at 8956 Pine Wood Drive, the nice neighborhood where the trees are big and the grass is nice and green and everyone has a pretty, big house, swimming pool and nice cars in their driveway. It's so quiet I thought to myself. I don't see any kids outside. Well, let's see how this is going to turn out. Am I going to like living here or will I hate staying here. Ms. Whitefield said well we are here. Are you ok, I said no. She said what's wrong? I said I miss my mom and I miss my dad. So the HRS lady reached over and gave me a hug and said it's ok. You will be ok. Your mommy is fine and your daddy will be here next weekend. As I sat there with water in my eyes wanting to cry, but thinking if I cried too much they might have to take me back to my mother or Mrs. Kent and her husband might not want me to stay at their house. So as we get out the car, the HRS lady rang the doorbell. Mr. and Mrs. Kent opened the door and said yes hello Kashia as I slowly looked up at them and said hi. Mrs. Kent said come in. As we entered their house, Mrs. Kent's little dogs came out and started barking at me. I hid behind the HRS lady and started crying. Mr. Kent told the dog to be quiet and then he looked at me and said come on they not going to mess with you. So the HRS lady came on in and we sat down. They were talking and letting them know that my dad would come get me on the weekends if it's ok with them I was saying to myself what you mean if it's ok with them that's my daddy. Mrs. Kent and the HRS lady walked around the house and Mrs. Kant showed her where I would be sleeping and my clothes and toys. The HRS lady got ready to leave and she looked at me and said I will be back to visit you in a few weeks. I replied ok. So then Mr. and Mrs. Kent showed me the house. We were already in the kitchen. It looked like a kitchen that was in the magazines.

So they show me the den; it was nice. Then they showed me the living room. It was so big and everything was glass. I couldn't go in there until Christmas time. Then they showed me my bathroom. As we walked in, I was like wow, that bathroom was so big you could fit me and ten other kids in there. Then they showed me Mr. Kent's office in the house. That was off limits. I couldn't go in there. Even Mrs. Kent couldn't go in there. I don't know that's what I said to myself. They show me their room, the master bedroom. They had their own bathroom and their own walk-in closet. They said if you ever get scared you can come get in the bed with us. Then they showed me my room. Oh my god. It was so big that it looked like a master bedroom just without the bathroom. I had a walk-in closet with new clothes and new shoes and all kind of toys. I had bunk beds and a TV in my room. I knew this was heaven. I thought I was in heaven. It was so pretty in there and it smelled so good. It had had two big photos of Mickey Mouse on the wall. One of the photos said welcome home and the other said I love you so much. I began to cry, not because I was sad, but because I was so happy. So I hugged Mr. and Mrs. Kent again and said thank you so much, I love you all while hugging me back they said we love you too. That night came and Mrs. Kent came in and gave me a bath and talked to me and let me know whatever I needed she would do her best to get it for me. I got ready for bed she asked me if I wanted to sleep with them or sleep in my room. I choose to sleep in my room because I just wanted to cry all night long. I was mad at my mom, but I missed her too. I really wanted to go home, but I knew if I went home, my mom would beat me again. But as time went on, I stayed with Mrs. Kent and went to school during the week and went to my dad's house on the weekend. I would see Chantey at school, but she wouldn't talk to me. She would say bad things about me to her friends. One day I just got tired of her saying bad things about me and I went up to her and called her a bald headed ape. She got mad and pushed me. I just remember hitting her in her face, pulling her hair and cursing her out and telling her I don't like you or your mama, I wish you and her would die. As we both got sent to the office, we got in trouble and got three licks with the paddle. I was mad and angry because I remembered my uncle hitting me with a paddle even though his paddle was ten times bigger than the school's and made marks on my butt. After we fought and got in trouble, we told each other we were sorry and hugged and went back to class. Time went on. I'm still going to my dad's house on the weekend and waiting on the courts to tell me I can go stay with my dad. While I waited Mrs. Kent and her husband taught me how to swim. I began to make friends in my neighborhood. Me and a girl Kim had become best of friends. I found out later that she went to my school. I was having the time of my life. No one was yelling at me.

No one was beating on me. I was good. I was enjoying myself, but on the inside, I missed my mother. I wanted to see her, but I knew she was still mad at me for what I did. By Christmas I had been there for almost a year. I had seen the photos on the wall of Mr. and Mrs. Kent kids but I had never met them. I had just talked to them on the phone. The Kent's kids came down for Christmas.

It was a wonderful time. Mrs. Ken's kids brought me all kind of clothes and toys. They were so nice to me. They had kids of their own, so me and their kids just played and played. If I wasn't black, you would think I was some kin to them, because we got along so well. On Christmas morning, I opened up all my gifts and I was so happy because I got stuff I didn't know existed. As we cleaned up all the paper, the door bell rang. It was my dad. Mrs. Kent didn't tell me my dad was coming. I was so happy I thought I was going with him that day, but I wasn't. I opened up the gifts he brought me and as sat for a while with him and my little brother. We laughed. We talked. We cried. I wanted to go with him. Little did I know, I would be going home with him soon. After my dad and my brother left, I went and got in Mr. and Mrs. Kent's bed and asked Mr. Kent why didn't my mom come see me. Is she still mad at me. Mr. Kent looked at me and said no your mommy loves you, she just can't come over until the judge says she can. I said ok and I got up and went in my room and played with my toys and just kept to myself asked myself what do. Christmas is over. I sit daily playing with my toys and waiting to go back to school. We get a knock at the door. It's the HRS lady, but this time, she had another little girl, Heidi, with her. Heidi had been abused by her mother and father.

She had been raped, but at the time I didn't know what rape meant. All I knew is that little girl looked just like me when I came to the Kent's house. Something on the inside of me really didn't want her there because now I would have to share the people who had been my parents for a year. I would also have to share my toys and my room and now all eyes would not be on me. I was mad and I didn't want to be there anymore. I began to act out.

I wouldn't play with Heidi. I would be mean to her because she was taking my parents. She began crying and trying to tell me why she was there and what happened to her. She told me how her mother burned her hand on the stove for being bad and how her dad burned her with the iron because she would cry when he got on top of her. I asked her why did he get on top on you? She said to have sex with me. I looked at her crazy because I didn't know what sex was. I was just in the 3rd grade. I didn't know what that was but I was to find out soon. She said I will show you. She said lay back, I will show you. She pulled her pants down, climbed on top of me and started moving up and down on me. I still didn't know what it meant because it didn't hurt. I asked her why did she cry, that didn't hurt.

She said because his penis was in me. Once again I was lost because I had never gone though that and my mother hadn't taught me that before I ran away. She said look at my finger, it is a penis. She took her hands, pulled on my dress and pulled my underwear to the side. She told me to open my legs, took her finger and put it inside me. I began to cry and yell. My foster mother came in and saw her and she yelled at her and told her not to do that. It was then I learned about sex and that nobody is supposed to touch you on your chest, or your butt, or where Heidi touched me. Mr. and Mrs. Kent were so mad at her, they called HRS. The HRS lady came out that day and talked to me and Heidi. They were getting ready to take her to another foster home, but Heidi started crying and said she was just showing me what her dad had done to her. They came and talked to me and I told them that she was showing me what her dad had done to her. The HRS lady said ok, but if that happens again let me know and I will remove her from here. Everything was good that night, but I remembered what she had done. When she made me mad, I would tease her and make fun of her for getting raped. I knew that would make her cry and leave me alone. I didn't know I would have to go through the same thing later in life with a someone in my family. So time went on and one day I was standing in the den with my toy microphone singing and looking at myself in the glass door. That that was my favorite toy. I loved singing. On this day I was just singing away when the door bell rang. It was the HRS lady and in my head I was saying whose coming now. She came in and she talked to talk to Mr. and Mrs. Kent who were crying. I didn't know why they were crying, so I stood there with water in my eyes, then I ran into living room and asked Mr. and Mrs. Kent why were they crying. Mrs. Kent grabbed me and started hugging me and Mr. Kent just started rubbing me on my back. They looked at me and said your dad is coming to get you. You're going to live with him. I was happy. I looked at them and said don't cry, I will come visit you if that's ok. They smiled and said they would love that. I smiled at them and told them I loved them. The HRS lady began to cry. I looked at her and said are you going to miss me too. She said you bet kid o. I gave her a hug and ran in the back to tell Heidi I was going with my dad. She looked at me and with a loud voice she said, "SO I DON'T CARE I HATE YOU!" I didn't know what I had done, so I started crying and told Mrs. Kent. Mrs. Kent said she didn't mean it, she was just upset. I went back in the room and gave her a hug and said I would be back to see her. She smiled and said I better.

The HRS lady left. Mrs. Kent went into the room to help me pack because my dad was coming to get me in the morning. I was up bright and early in the morning. Mrs. Kent got up and made me some bacon, pancakes and eggs. She said good morning dear your last morning here with us I will miss you. You need to know we love you and you are always welcome to come here or to call. I put my address and my phone number in your bag if you ever want to call me or Mr. Kent. I smiled and said I will be back to see you all. She looked at me as if she knew once I walked out those doors I wasn't coming back. As I sat there eating, the door bell rang. I jumped up and down saying my daddy is here. Mrs. Kent opened the door and said hi Mr. King how are you? He said good even better I get to bring my little girl home with me. Mrs. Kent tried to hold back her tears, but as I looked up at her, her eyes was filled with water. I gave her a hug and told her don't cry, I will be back. As she and my dad packed his car with my stuff, I ran in the back to hug Mr. Kent. He was sitting on the side of the bed with tears in his eyes and said, I love you come back and see us. I looked at him and said I will. Don't cry. Good bye. I went in the room where Heidi was and she was laying in the bed mad. I looked at her and said, don't be mad. I will be back to see you and play with you ok. She said, no you won't, you will forget about me. I said no I won't, I promise. She got up out of the bed and hugged me and gave me a kiss on my cheek. So as I walked out I looked back at her and blew her a kiss and said I love you. I headed out to the car and Mrs. Kent hugged me again and said be good, I love you. I said I will, I love you. My dad smiled and said thank you for everything you did for my baby girl. He gave Mrs. Kent a hug and we got in the car and left. I am at my dad house with my brother and all my family members on my dad side. When I got there, there were a lot of people there-- my dad's sister, s my dad's brothers, cousins--with the grill going and all kind of food and drinks. As we pulled up in the yard everybody started running up to the car trying to get me out the car and hugging me. I was so happy. I felt like a star because it was all about me. So as I began my life with my dad staying at my 's house with my little brother, I was loving life. I got to do and go anywhere I wanted. I stayed with my dad about three years. My dad's sister, Theresa, was real sick.

 She had breast cancer and we would go visit her daily. This sister and my mom were real close. One day my dad had got a phone call telling him his sister had died. , As days went by, my dad's sister's husband began to get ready for the funeral. On the day of the funeral, I saw my mother. She looked up and saw me and smiled and waved. I let my dad's hand go and I ran over to my mother. I hugged her and said I love you mommy. She looked at me and gave me a half of a hug and said I love you. I rode with her to the gravesite and stood there holding her hand just as happy as I could be. I wanted to go home with her, but still I didn't know if she was going to be mad at me or not. I didn't care; I was just glad to see her. After the funeral I asked my mother if I could go with her and she said she didn't care and to ask my dad. I ran back to my dad saying dad come here. Mom is here. Can I go with mom please.

He said where. I said to her house. I asked him as my mom was walking up to him. As she got there she said in a real funny voice, hi Stony. As he spoke, he looked my mom up and down as if he were falling back in love with her all over again. So my dad said I could go with my mom. I hung out with her all day. We went to McDonald's and ate and went over Mrs. Ross's house and some more of my mother friend's house's. She called my grandmother and let me talk to my granny, my auntie and my uncles. My granny asked me if I wanted to come to Mobile for Christmas. I said yes. I was happy because everybody was being nice to me and wanted to see me. So my mom took me back home to my dad and she asked him could I go to Mobile for the Christmas break. My dad said sure just let him know.

Chapter 6

Here I am Again

I was with my mom on the way to granny's house. As we drove the long highway going 75 north to Mobile, I was so excited because I hadn't seen my granny, my auntie, my cousin, my uncles and all the people who knew me in Mobile. You might think I would be scared to come up here, but I'm not because I felt I made a point to my family when I ran away from home. So as we rode all day my mom was so nice to me. She didn't yell or say nothing mean. It was just so nice and I was really thinking about coming back home because my mom had changed. At least that was what I thought, but it was just a front because I was just with her for the weekend. I had go back Sunday night and she didn't want me to tell my dad! We pulled up at granny's house. The big green house still looked the same outside. Mom asked, do you know where you at? I said yes at granny's. I jumped out of the car to run in the house to see granny, my auntie, and my uncles. They ran outside to hug and kiss me. They were so happy to see me. As my auntie cried and held me tight and said, I love you girl you are so big and so pretty. She turned to my mom and said Red she so (d***) pretty. My uncle Mike ran out and said there is my baby look at you. You're so big and pretty, you look just like your mother, red just like her, short just like her, pretty just like her. You're going to break some man's heart. Little did I know he was giving me all the compliments because he wanted me in a sexual way. But I smiled and in my head wanted to come back down here with my granny. I had forgotten that I got beat with a bid wood paddle. I had forgiven my granny for talking about my dad and yelling and cursing at me. I just wanted to come back down here. We walked towards the house.

My cousins ran outside yelling my cousin's home and giving me hugs and kisses. If only someone would have told me I was going to be their sex toy I would have stayed where I was. But, as I got closer to the house I didn't see granny. So I asked where granny was? My auntie said oh granny had gone to bingo. My mother said ok move. Let me hide the car in the back yard so she won't know we're here. So my mom hid the car in the back. We were in the house looking at TV and granny turned that corner on two wheels. My auntie said there is mama right there. Me and my mama ran in the back room and hid from granny. Granny pulled up in the yard, got out of her van and ran into the house because she had to pee real bad. She got in the house and ran to the bathroom without looking out back. When she got done, she got up and looked out her bathroom window and said who's car. As she paused me and my mother ran in the bathroom. I said hi granny and she screamed. She said there is my grandbaby and hugged me. We went downstairs and I sat in granny's lap and talked to her. She began to ask me stuff and I could tell somebody had to told my mom not to ask me anything about the past because as my granny got ready to ask me something, my mom would look at her mother and shake her head. And Granny wouldn't ask me anything. But then my granny asked me the magic words, DO YOU WANT TO COME STAY WITH ME! As I sat on her lap and smiled and said yes, she said when you get home ask your dad if can you come stay with granny. I said yes ma'am. I enjoyed Christmas with my mom and my granny in Mobile. Everything was good and fine. As the weekend came to an end, my mom and I got ready to go back to Gainesville. I began to cry because I didn't want to go back home with my dad. I wanted to stay with my granny and my mother. We were going on 75 south back home and I began to talk with my mom about going back home with her. She said, you need to know if you are bad, you will get a whipping. I said yes ma'am. Then she began to ask me how I liked staying with my dad, if I got what I needed from my dad and was it everything I thought it would be. So I began to say things to my mom that were mean about my dad because I wanted to go her home with her even thou my dad didn't do anything. He treated me like his little girl, but I just made up stuff because I wanted go home with my mother. I returned home with my dad.

When I got back home that night, my dad and his family were over to the house playing cards, eating and drinking as they do every weekend. As I got ready to get out the car, my dad walked outside and spoke to my mother. He asked me did I have fun. I said yes and then I said daddy, I want to go stay with mommy. He looked at me as if I had stuck a knife in his heart. With a soft voice he said yes you can go stay the night with your mother on the weekends. I said no daddy I want to go stay with mommy and go to school with mommy. My dad looked at my mom as if he wanted to hit her. But, he just went to the back of my mom's car and began getting my stuff out her car.

He looked at me and said we will talk about this later honey ok. So I ran around the car to hug my mom and tell her I loved her. She smiled and said I love you too. Mommy will see you soon . She got in her car my dad told me to go in the house while he talked to my mother.

I did and I didn't hear what my mom and dad said, but I knew they had said some mean words to each other. When my dad came back in the house, he came in my room with a loud voice and said, YOU WILL NOT BE GOING TO STAY WITH YOUR MOTHER EVER. As I stood there with water in my eyes, mad and sad I began to look at my dad and say in my mind oh yes I'm and you can't stop me. So as time went on I would be bad in school, talk back to my dad, and beat up my little brother. I started to mess with his family. I had them hating one another. I would do all this stuff so my dad would let me go stay with my mother. One weekend my dad let me spend the night with my mom. I thought we were going back to the old house and my old room. I was happy. We were riding and riding and riding. We passed by the old house and I said, mom, where are we going you passed by the house. She looked at me, smiled and said baby I don't stay there anymore. I stay in Miami. So as we get to Miami, we pull up to a big apartment complex with a big gate around it. There was a key pad to get in. We pulled up to my mom's apartment. She opened the door and we walked into a big living room.

To the right was my mom's room with her own bathroom and walk-in closet. To the left was my room with my own bathroom and a walk-in closet. What, a girl my age with my own bathroom and walk-in closet. It was as if my mother knew I was coming back home. She had my bunk bed in the room, all my dolls and clothes. Everything in that room was fixed up like my old room. It was just bigger. I had a bathroom in my room and my clothes were too little for me because I had gotten fat. Everything was right. My mom was acting nicer. We were in a new town. My mom was a CO correctional officer, so now she knew right from wrong. She worked for the police, so now she knew she couldn't beat me like she used to. I was real happy and ready to move back home with my mom. Everything looked and sounded good. Throughout the weekend, my mom and I did all kinds of stuff like a mother and daughter should. We had girl talk. She asked me about my dad and if anybody was doing anything to me in a bad way. I replied no ma'am. She began to tell me about the birds and the bees and that no one was supposed to touch me in my private parts. The weekend ended and I was sad because I didn't want to leave. My mom saw I was sad and had water in my eyes.

She began to tell me that I bought this on myself because I ran away. She said she would talk to my dad. I said ok. So we got ready to leave to go back to Gainesville to my dad. When we got back to my dad once I again I say dad mom got a big house in Miami and I want to go stay with my mom. This time my dad acted as if he didn't hear me. I looked at my mom and said ok mom love you, I will see you soon. She had this look in her eye like I know because you getting ready to do something wrong. She remembered that look I had the day I ran away from school. I looked at her with that same look she knew I was getting ready to do something, but she just looked and said ok baby, see you soon. As the week went on, I got worse I did not listen to my dad. He told me he knew why I was acting up, but I was not going to stay with my mom. Little did I know that the only reason he didn't want me to leave was because the state would cut half of his food stamps. I heard him and my auntie talking about it when they thought I was outside, but I was in my room and heard everything. I knew I had to step up my game. I wasn't getting beat so the HRS lady wouldn't come get me and take me back to my mom's house. My mom moved to Miami so I couldn't run away from school. I had to think real hard. I know you might be thinking what does a nine-year old know about getting deeper in her thoughts? But, I was a little girl with the mind of a grown woman. So for two weeks straight I got in trouble at school and did stuff so my dad could whip me. I got suspended from school. My dad was very mad and whipped me.

When he did, I cried and I told him I hated him and I didn't love him and I did not want to stay with him anymore. I wanted to stay with my mother. My dad was real mad at me and he said I'm going to pack your (s***) and take you to your mother. And when she starts beating you again, do not call me and do not come back because I have been good to you. I have given you everything you wanted, but I guess that ain't good enough for you. Get your stuff and get back over there with your mother. As I stood there with madness in my heart, I started acting like my mother. I got smart with my dad and started talking back to him. I told him my mother was not going to hit me anymore because she was a police officer. I said I didn't care if he didn't want me to come back. That was when my dad jumped up and slapped me across my face and said get away from me. I began to cry and stomped off. That day he called my mom and said Kashia has one more week in school before the summer, but she got kicked out for the rest of the year, so you can come get her. She is going to live back with you. You got what you want. I will meet you to bring her to you. My mom laughed and said I didn't tell her to do anything.

She just wanted to come live with me. She said if I were you, I would have whipped her butt. My dad said I did, but I can't deal with this. I will have all her paperwork and her stuff and I'm bringing her to you. In Miami with my mom, she worked mornings, which was fine because I could stay at her friend's house in the morning and be with her in the evening and night. So the school year is back in. I started school and I loved being with my mom. I still got in trouble, but not as bad as I was. I would still get whippings, but not as bad. Plus, I wasn't get hit in my face anymore. I still got hit with a belt or I might get hit up side my head. Sometimes my mom would yell and it would make me cry because now she was is a corrections office. I didn't have family in Miami to run to and she would tell me if I ran away I would be put in jail. I believed that because she worked for them. She would have the police officers that worked on her job come by the house and tell me the same thing. Her friend Fred he would take me to the jail and walk me around when I got in trouble at home. He told me if I kept being bad, her would bring me to jail. I was scared. As time went on, I went to school and passed. I would go stay with granny for the summer. Because my granny would go to bingo, I would have to stay with my uncle Mike and his boys. I was there with them and my uncle gave me baths. Let me remind you I was in the sixth grade and had just passed to the seventh. I was eleven years old, but he gave baths. As he bathed me, he is rubbed me and put his hands where he had no business. Now I'm really scared because I remembered what Heidi did to me when I stayed in foster care. I thought about what my mom said about people touching me in my practice parts. So I'm scared and mad and don't know what to do. If I cry or holler, I would get beat by my uncle or I would have to go back to foster care. I sat there looking crazy and my uncle said to me that he had to clean me down there and make sure I was clean. He looked at me with a smile and said you know you are uncle's baby and I love you. It's alright for me to touch you down there. He kissed me on my lips and took his hands, put them in the water and rubbed on me. Now I knew this was not right because Heidi's dad did it to her and she cried and had to come to foster care. I sat there not saying anything. I was scared and mad at him. And if that were not enough, he would dry me off and put powder on his hands and rub across my chest while smiling and saying you so pretty niece, I love you. He would give me one of his big t-shirts and tell me to get in his bed. He would get in bed with me, pull me close to him and put his penis on my butt. My grandmother would call and tell him she was home and to bring me to her. He would get mad at my granny yell. I was happy because I did not want him touching me anymore.

Before I left, he would tell me he didn't do anything wrong and if I told anyone, he would get his board and beat me and he wouldn't love me anymore. I wouldn't be his baby and he would stop buying me things. I thought he would hate me, so at first, I didn't say anything to anyone. So now school was starting back and I'm getting ready to go back home. Thank God. As school began, I was back at school and enjoying life. As the school year went on, everything was good. Life was good. I was getting ready to turn twelve. My mom was working morning shifts until one day my mom's boss came to her with an open night position where she would make money and be full time with full time benefits. She said you know I have my daughter, but I will get back to you in three days. She did and told her boss she would take the night job. School was getting ready to be out again for the summer and I could go and stay with my Granny until I was old enough to stay at home by myself. As she called my granny and told her what was going on, I heard and I was getting mad. I didn't want to go. She got off the phone with my grandmother and began to tell me the plans as far me going to my granny's house and me going to school. As I sat there crying and saying I didn't want to go, she began to ask me why I didn't want to go and I didn't say anything. I just said I don't want to live down there with them. My mother said I did not have a choice because she had to work the night shift and no one would be at home with me. She didn't have the money to have someone to keep me. I had no choice but to go. So I told my mom when I go to granny would she tell granny not to send me over to my uncle house anymore. She asked why and said I didn't want to get beat or sent back to foster care and my dad said I could not come back. I lied to my mother and said he was hitting me with that board. My mom asked why I didn't say nothing before. I just stood there and said I don't know. She said don't worry about it, I would not be going over there anymore and if he touched me again she would have him put in jail. No one was to hit me, but granny. So my mother called granny and told her what I had said. But, I was scared because I was lying about him hitting me. The truth he was touching me in places my mother said no one was to touch me.

Chapter 7
Why Me?

I was at granny's house. My life as a child was no more. This was where I really found out who I was, the rough side of me --the spirits of hate, lying, sex, all eyes on me, fighting, stealing. I just plain acted out for attention because I was hurt I wanted everybody else to hurt. I didn't care who it was. I was at granny's house and mom told my granny I was not to go over Mike house anymore because if he hit me or did anything to me, she would bury Mike and she would going to jail. My granny looked at me and asked what did Mike do to me that I couldn't have told her. I wanted to tell, but I knew if I told I could have gone back to Mrs. Kent house. I said nothing except he hit me and he hits people with that board. Granny believed me because he had been hitting his kids with the board and had even broken my cousin's arm which was why my cousin was now staying with my granny. Granny said that was not a problem, I would not be going over there. I was so happy. I felt like I did not have to say anything because I did not have to be around Mike. Little did I know it was not over that sex demon was sitting there all along. So as I got ready to leave to go to work my uncle came in the house and said there she is, my niece with her pretty self. He looked at me as if I were a woman of his age or something. So my mom said, my child told me what you did. His eyes got big and he looked at me as if he wanted to kill me. He raised his voice and said, what did I do to your child or what lie has she told you. My mom looked at me as if she suspected something else because of the way he was acting. But, just said, you were hitting her with that paddle you have. No one hits her but my mother and me.

I had her, not you. She is my child and if you hit her and I find out about it, it's on. He looked at me and said, well if that's how you feel, don't come to my house. Don't ask me for nothing. You are no kin to me. I don't like you and when your mommy goes to bingo, don't send her over my house to watch her. My mom, my granny and my uncles had words, and my uncle got mad and left. I was happy. I knew I did not have to worry about him anymore. That was when I knew I had a hate problem. Every time he came around, I didn't speak to him. I didn't hold any words with him and I wish he were dead. I hated him for the things he did to me. I hated him he for the things he said to me and about me. So here I was. me, my cousin, my auntie and her kids, and, my uncle George. My uncle KG was in jail. My uncle Robert stayed out of town and my uncle Earl was married and living with his wife and child. So I started school. Granny was going to bingo a lot, so I was left with my aunt and uncle. But, because they sold drugs, they would stay gone and be around the corner which left me with my uncle Mike kids who were older than me. One day granny went to bingo, my aunt and uncle had left and we were at home by ourselves. It started out with them just hitting me and fighting me. I would cry and they would say if I told, they would tell granny I went outside or I ate her cookies.

Whatever I had done they would threaten to tell so I would get whipping. The next time I was left at home with them they hit me harder. I had bruises on my back, leg and arm. I didn't know why they were hitting me. I thought it was to make me tough, but it wasn't. As time went on, granny's house got kicked in again by the police.

This time they found drugs. My aunt was at home, but my uncle was not there. When the police found the drugs and asked whose it was, my aunt said it was hers. She said it so granny would not go to jail or have her house taken and us placed in foster care. My aunt went to jail. It was me, my auntie's two boys, my uncle Mike's two boys and my uncle living in the house. So once again granny went to bingo and uncle went around the corner to sell drugs. I was left at home with my older cousins to beat me. I was mad I didn't want to be there.

They would say little stuff to me to make me mad so we could fight. So this day as I was fighting my cousins, my cousin Cedi told his brother Benson to bring me in the back and hold me down. As his brother did it, I was yelling and crying for them to stop. Cedi pulled down his clothes and pulled up my dress and began to stick his penis in me. I screamed and yelled for him to stop. He began to hit me and called me a (b****) and told me to shut up. At that time his brother Benson told him to move and let him get some. Cedi got up and Benson pulled his pants down and got on top of me and stuck his penis inside me. I screamed and yelled for him to stop. He was hurting me. They hit me in the face and told me to shut up or they would kill me. My cousin Cedi went in the kitchen and got a knife and held it to my face. He said, do you see this little (b****). I will kill you if you don't shut up and if you tell anybody I will kill you in your sleep. So I just laid there crying and bleeding as they got done doing their business. When my granny got home, I wanted to go tell her. I went and sat on the couch next to her and told her I wanted to go home. She asked me why what was wrong. My cousin Cedi came from out the kitchen and stood in the doorway of the den with the knife in his hand

and said under his breath if I said anything he was going to kill me. I looked at granny and I said nothing, I just wanted my mother. The next day my granny left and my uncle left. I was again in the house with my cousins by myself. They beat me. And because I told my granny I was ready to go home, they raped me. This time when they raped me, they held me down on my stomach and pulled my pants down. They got the hair grease, rubbed it on their penises and they stuck me in my butt. I laid there again screaming and yelling and crying for them to stop. They laughed and said shut up. I would know the next time to keep my mouth closed. I laid there and said I did not tell, I just wanted to go home. They told me I wasn't going home. My mother didn't want me.

She hated me and didn't love me. That was why she brought me there. They called me all kind of names and beat me while I was laying down. So now I have a spirit of sex. Every day when my grandmother would go to bingo or to the store, she would leave me with my cousins. They raped and beat me. They made me give them oral sex. Sometimes she would be downstairs and they would hit me in my head or in my face and make me give them oral sex. All they were doing was feeding that sex demon. I began losing myself. I didn't care about myself. I would get pens and stick my arms trying to kill myself. I would look at myself in the mirror and start hitting myself in the face. I would eat and eat to find comfort because I knew I could not tell anyone or they would kill me. I would be dead or staying with another family and I didn't want that. So, what I did was stop crying about it when they raped me. I began to come in the room when I granny leave and pull my clothes off and have sex with them as if we were lovers. We would have sex every day, sometimes two or four times a day because that sex demon had me feeling like I needed it. I had to have it and it was love. If I just gave them me, they would not beat me.

I could do what I wanted and get away with it because they won't tell on me because I was giving them what they wanted. I began to lie about my age to my cousin's friends so I could sleep with them. I felt sex was the only way I could get someone to love me and take up for me. Anytime my granny or uncle or anybody said anything to me, my cousin would take up for me. All the beatings I should have gotten for being bad, or whatever the case was, I did not because my cousin would not let me get in trouble. So now I'm feeding my hate demon. I'm feeding my lying demon. I'm feeding my sex demon. I'm feeding my all eyes on me demon. Every day I had on a short dress and a push up bra with tissues in it making me older. I was just thirteen. I was doing me all the way, but on the inside I was so hurt and wished someone could see me for who I really was. I wished someone would come and rescue me from this hell hole. I started hating my mom and telling myself it was her fault that I was like this because she made me come down here and I didn't want to come. When she called I did not have much to say to her. In my mind I wanted to tell her I hate you and I'm a (w****) because of you. I hate myself because of you. I'm dressing like this because of you. But all I could do was give her short talk and be mad at her. One day my granny went to the store.

Benson was sleep. Me and Cedi were up laying in granny's bed. We heard the door close as she said she would be back. We thought she was going to bingo, but she was going to the store. Me and Cedi began having sex. My grandmother pulled in, but we did not hear her so as she came in the house and came up stairs, she walked in the room and caught us having sex. She began yelling and hit us for a moment. I was so happy she caught us so they would stop having sex with me. One part of me was mad that she caught us because that meant no more sex for me and I wouldn't be able to feed my hunger for sex.

The day she caught us, she told Joe to go and get her so switches and put them together because she was getting ready to beat us like never before. After she beat us, she called my mother. My mother cursed me and asked if Benson was having sex with me. I paused then said no because I didn't want to get him in trouble. After my mother got off the phone with me, my granny asked if she wanted to talk to Cedi. My mother said no, she wanted to kill him for touching me. Then she said something I would never forget. She told my granny, you got her now. Do what you want. I don't care, she can't run away to her daddy's house. As I heard her say that, my heart got heavy and I really began to hate her because now everything my cousins said that day they had me held down was true. She didn't care about me. She didn't love me.

Now she just added gas to the fire. Since she didn't care, I was going to keep on doing what I was doing. I was going to get pregnant because I needed someone to love me, because no one loved me. My uncle comes over and my granny told him what happened. He looked at me and began to call me all kind of (w****) and names. He went in his car and got his board and beat me and my cousin until our butts bled. My mother did nothing and told my uncle he needed to beat me. I heard that and I got even madder. I put him out and said I don't know why you're beating me. You used to touch me when I stayed over your house. Granny got up from her seat and slapped me in my face called me all kinds of names and said I was a lie and if I told somebody else that she would beat me and put me out on the streets. My uncle looked at me and said he did not touch me. I was family. He said that since I wanted to lie not to say anything to him anymore. He would kill me. My mother sat on the phone crying and mad not saying anything. She wanted to believe me, but didn't know what to think. My grandmother made it seem like I just hot in the pants. So now, I hate everybody in this house .I want to just go and jump off a bridge somewhere. Time still went on. My mom wasn't really talking to me. My granny really did not have anything to me. So here I was doing what I wanted. When she left for bingo, I still had sex with my cousins and their best friends hoping one of them would get me pregnant so I could have a child of my own. I wanted someone to love and someone to love me back.

Chapter 8

The love or lust I just need it.

I was fifteen years old and in the 9th grade. I left Mobile and had to start a new school in the middle of the school year,. I was mad as hell because I had to leave all my friends and leave the food that was feeding my sex demon. I got to stay with my mother, which by the way she really did not want to be around me, but that was cool because I didn't want to be around her. So now I'm not only mad about leaving Mobile, but I'm scared all over because I know if I mess up I will be beat and I won't have a place to run or hide and no one to take up for me. I was starting a new school in the middle of the year, high school at that, and I did not know anyone.

So I know for sure now I want get pregnant and have a child of my own. Because my mother is not going to let me go anywhere or do anything. I'm not only in hell, but I'm hell with gas on my drawers. Great. On Friday morning me and my mother were at the school, Dr. Tiles High School, getting my paperwork together so I could start school. As we sat there in the office and my mom filled out paperwork, I thought about Mobile and what could do so she would send me back. So as the guidance teacher talked to me, I sat and listened. She looked at my grades and asked if I was in the special classes. I looked at her and told her no because I didn't want to be the new kid in the dumb classes. I lied and said no. Because I lied that caused me to be in all the honor classes because the grades on my report card were A's and B's. I'm the new girl on the block in honor classes with the nice body and nice fitting clothes, with long pretty skill weave and pretty skin with my make-up on on the outside.

But hurting and mad my body is over heated for sex on the inside. The teacher asked my mother if I was going to start today or on Monday. My mom said I would start today. I thought to myself, you are off today I could have waited until Monday and we could spend this time together like a mother and daughter. So I looked at her and tried to hold back my tears because she really don't want me around her. We sat there and waited on the teacher to get done with my schedule. My mom began to look at the paper and write down the teacher's name and number. She gave her numbers because she wanted them to let her know if they had a problem with me so she could beat me. But it was ok because I did not want to be there. I was missing Mobile and I wished she would have just left me there or just send me back. Because I found out the real reason I was there was because she was trying to put my dad on child support and the only way she could get it was if I was living with her. I was her meal ticket. So the teacher took me to my first class and as she opened the door my heart dropped because all eyes were on me, the new girl. I went up to my English teacher, Mr.Wilkos, as he said hi and introduced me to the class. Everyone was happy and so nice. I loosened up a little. One of the girls said, hey new girl, you can come sit with me. I will help you find your classes. As I looked at this little girl, I noticed the way she was acting was how I was feeling on the inside-- loud, wanting to be seen and heard, loved sex, wild and out, and just really didn't care who knew it. So as the day went on, she took me to my classes. Everything was cool. As my body got hotter and hotter, I looked at the boys there. There were a lot of mixed and light skinned kids in my classes and I was into mixed and light boys. I sat in my class and looked at them but really did not want them because I only did older boys. I did not care if they were one year older than me or ten years older than me, I just couldn't do any one the same age or in the same grade as me. All day the boys in my class were trying to talk to me. I just looked at them because I wanted someone older that was already having sex and that would be able to come over my mother's house while she was not there at night. I wasn't looking for a boyfriend, just someone to have sex with me. That day was over.

I still really did not know anyone and was glad to go home and get locked up in my room. I wouldn't have to see my mother and she wouldn't have to see me. So the weekend is here and she is at work. I'm out side where I'm not supposed to be, but I'm out there because I'm looking for sex and don't care where it comes from. As soon as I open my door, my mom's best friend Ms. Nikki is sitting there with her kids. My mom has already told her the deal, so she says hi honey what are you doing outside. I said just standing here looking. How are you. But, in my head I said ok she is a nosey (b****). She called her kids outside and said these are my kids Jon and Rita. They go to Dr. Tiles too. I stood there and said, oh ok. I really didn't care because her son was in the same grade as me, and his sister was a white girl in a black girl's body. That was not going to work. She said Monday, I will show you where the bus stop is. We leave the house at 6:35 am. The bus will be there at 6:55 am. I said ok, but I really didn't care right then. I had sex on my mind. The demon was hungry and I needed to feed it. I was about to lose my mind. I went back in the house and went to my room. I laid there trying to find out how I was going to feed my demon. I began to cry and I cried myself to sleep. So this was going on all weekend. I was about to lose it. I really hated my mother because I didn't have anything any friends, no boys, no nothing. On Monday at 5:25 am, my mom came in my room and woke me up. I looked at her and said do I have to go. She looked at me and says (h***) yes, you have to get up out of here. I got up and went the bathroom and washed my face, brushed my teeth, pulled my hair up in chop sticks and put my make-up on . I looked like a little china doll. I had a nice dress that showed my legs all shiny. I had cute sandals on, my nails were done, my feet were done and I had some of my mother's perfume on. I walked out into the kitchen to get the money that my mother gave me to eat lunch with. Jon and Rita knocked on my door. I grabbed my book bag and told my mother, ok mom I'm gone. She said, ok I will see you later. Lock the door behind you. I walked outside to the gate at the end of the road. I saw all these different people at the bus stop. They looked at me and asked if I was the new girl that stayed in 402. I said yes. The older boys stood there ready for whatever and tried to see whose girlfriend I was going to be. But they were really scared because they knew my mother and where she worked. They didn't want to say too much because they were older than me and they didn't' want to go to jail. The bus arrived and I put in my mind that today would be the day I would be getting me some. It was time to let my hair down because I needed someone while I was here in this hell hole. We get to school. The high school was split up. Ninth graders had their own campus and tenth through twelfth graders had their own campus. Some of the classes were on the 10th grade campus. Band, choir and PE classes were on the 10th-12th grade campus. So when I got off the bus, I got off on the big campus and walked to the 9th grade campus. As I walked, everybody wanted to know who I was and where I came come from. Rita, her brother and I continued to walk to the 9th grade campus, a girl named Leah looked at me and said Kashia. I looked at her and began screaming and yelling and hugging her and saying to myself thank God I know someone here. Rita and Jon stopped, but I told them they could go ahead. I knew Leah from middle school. I was happy. I knew she knew what I needed to know. We walked to our campus to the lunch room where I was introduced to all her friends and family. I talked to the loud girl from Friday and her other loud friend came over and spoke. I found out quickly they were very close. Even the loud girl and her friend could get me what I needed. My girl Leah was my friend and she was the ear I needed. She understood me. So that morning we went to our home rooms . First period we had math together. Mrs. Heart was our teacher. She was a black teacher. She was real and she was fun to be around. She talked to me and asked me for my paper to make sure I was in the right class. She looked at me and said, do you know Leah. I said yes ma'am. She said ok, I will let you sit by her, but I'm not going to have a problem out of you girls. I said no. Class began. Leah's cousin Paul was the same little boy that tried to talk to me Friday came up and said Leah is this your friend. Leah said yes and no you can't talk to her because you are a dog and I'm not going to let you talk to my girl and hurt her. I didn't say anything because I wasn't looking for a boyfriend. I really didn't want a dog as my sex partner. I had been done wrong so much that I didn't want anyone one using me or beating on me. I just smiled and didn't pay him any mind. My math teacher said, boy go sit down. You were just was in some other girl's face last week. So most of my classes I had with Leah, which was cool. I had a friend now, someone I could talk to. I still was missing that person to feed my sex demon. So as we went to lunch another one of Leah's cousins came up to us. He was in the 11th grade. He was the young man that stayed in my apartment complex. She introduced me. I said I knew who he was, smiled and gave him a sexual look. We talked. I didn't know he was looking for a girlfriend. We talked at lunch. As the day went on, every period he would come over and walk me to my next class as if we were a couple. It was ok at first because he was trying to get to know me and I was trying to have sex with him that day. So as the day ended, we got on the bus. We got to our bus stop and he began to walk with me. I was straight as I could be that day. I told him I wanted him to come over when my mom left home for work. He agreed and I told him I wanted him. He looked at me like what, for real. He said don't play with me man. I said I'm not playing as my body became real hot and wet for him. When I got home, my mom was there. She said how was your day. I said good, real good. I saw my friend Leah middle school. She said good, now you have someone to talk to and somebody's house you can go over to. I looked at her with this yeah right look because I knew I wasn't going anywhere. She said the food is on the stove. All you got to do is put the food in the microwave and warm your food up. I said ok. She got ready to leave. I was going to take a bath and get ready for Ken. I told him my mom left at 3:00 pm but wait until 4:00 so I would know she was at work. Once she was at work she couldn't leave. At 4:00 my door bell rang. Ken stood there looking like a thug. I let him in. As he began to talk I took him straight to my room and pulled off his clothes. He stopped and said wait, I've got to put this on. I looked at him and asked him why, I don't have anything. He said, I know I just don't want any kids. I was mad because that was what I wanted. But, because my body was hungry for sex. I said, ok let's do this. We laid there having sex. I was

74

laying there really not into it because once he said he
didn't want kids, he was not fulfilling what I needed him
to do. I was used to rough sex and being held down. He
wasn't doing any of that. When we got done I just looked
at him. He laid there saying what's wrong. I said nothing
you've got to go. He was like why your mom doesn't
come home until 11:00 tonight. I said I don't care you
have got to go. He began to get mad and started cursing
me out. I yelled back at him and told him he wasn't about
nothing in bed. He grabbed me and hit me in my face. I
told him he had to leave and not to walk me to my classes
anymore. He got mad and told me I was his and he would
have me. I got what I needed that day. It really made me
mad because I wanted more, just not with him. And if
that wasn't enough, I went to the park in my apartment
complex and met this guy that was always over there. I
didn't know him but I knew his sister. He was looking for
sex, not a girlfriend. I said that's what I need too. I wound
up sleeping with him. As I laid up with him I said that's
not what I wanted. I really wanted someone who was
going to love me and be there for me physically and
emotionally. I went to school every day. Ken would come
over to our campus and try to walk me to class. I would
look at him and say I don't want you. Get away from me.
I would make him look bad in front of my friends. He
would try to get back at me by telling them he slept with
me. I sat there saying, you're lying. I didn't do anything
with you. I told him if you did something with me, go and
tell my mother and let's see what see do. He left me alone
and never to talked to me. So weeks have passed and as
much as I have ridden this bus and gotten off this bus, I
never paid attend to this one boy on our bus. We had a
ghetto black bus driver and she was messy. One day me
and Leah were the first ones on the bus and we sat to the

back. The back is where all the higher class sat. We knew that I was looking for love, for one that could not only give me sex, but give it to me right, give me a baby and become my all in all. So as we sat there, Luke gets on the bus. Luke is 6'2" with real dark skin and a nice shape. He had pretty white teeth and looked like Jodi from the movie Baby Boy. I saw him; it was love at first sight. Leah says, "Hi Luke. What's up? Haven't see you in a minute." He replied and said, "I been riding home with my sister and her boyfriend." Luke looked at me and said, Hey how you doing?" I smile and said, "Fine." He said, "I can see that " He sat down in the seat with me. As he sat down, Ken got on the bus and looked at me and got mad. He walked back to the seat and asked Luke, what you doing man?.Luke looked at him and said my bad I didn't know this was you. You better hold onto her before I get her. I looked at Luke and said, we are not together. You can sit here. Ken looked me and said oh that's how you going to be?.I looked at him and said what did I tell you. He got mad and he said don't forget what I told you. Luke stepped in and said man, what's up. They had words. Luke walked up on Ken, Ken moved back and walked off calling me a (w****). Luke said, what did he tell you. I told him he said if he can't have me no one else could have me. So Luke told him make this your last time stepping to her because she's my girl. He left it at that because they all knew Ken was abusive and they thought that's why I didn't want to be with him. So that's how we left it. I really was in love now. Luke had said all the right things and he had taken up for me. All I needed was to see what he was like in bed. We were riding home just talking when he said can I come over and see you. I said yes. He said I don't want to do anything. I just want to get to know you since you are my girl now. I was excited and thought to myself this is the one. I might not have to leave now because I think I have just found my lover. So as we get off the bus, our bus driver says, this ain't your stop. Where are you going Luke. She smiled, I smiled and he smiled. So as we're all walking to the apartments, I looked at him and said, you can't come now my mom is home and she is crazy I can't have boys in my house. You can still walk with me so I can show you where to come and show you my mother's car so when you see it's gone you can come back. I showed him where I stayed and my mother's car. I told him to wait until 3:30 because she had to be to work at 3 and once she was there she couldn't leave. He waited at the park. I went in the house, said hi to my mother and went straight to the tub. She asked why I was taking a bath so early. I said I was hot and needed to take a bath. She said, Ok. Food is on the stove. You know what to do. I'm back tonight I might work until the morning. If I do, I will let you know. I said ok. I didn't care. My new lover was coming over. I took a bath and got ready for him When I got out of the tub, I put on a short skirt with a tank top and a push up bra that showed all my business. At 3:35 the doorbell rang. I made him wait five minutes. The doorbell rang again. I opened the door, He looked at me and said, "Wow! You look good girl. What's up with that." I smiled as he hugged me and kissed me on my neck and ear. He rubbed on me and made love to my lips as he kissed me as if I was his wife and he was my husband. So I told him to come. We sat down on the couch and talked and got to know each other. I told him parts of my life, not all because I didn't want to run him off, but I told him about my mom and my dad. He talked to me about his past and his family. He had family issues but they weren't as bad as mine. While we watched TV, I was all on him. That's when that sex demon kicked in and wanted him. But I thought he was nice and I didn't want him to think of me that way. I began to kiss him on his ear and his neck and I found out that was his hot spot. As I kissed on him, he began kissing on me. I straddled his lap still kissing on him. Then asked me if this was what I wanted. I said yes if this is what you want. He said it's on. I started kissing on him and pulling his shirt off. I loosened his pants. He picked me up and carried me to my bedroom. He laid me on my bed and undressed. He started at my neck kissing on my chest and said this is my heart, don't take it from me. My eyes got watery. He kept kissing me on my chest, down to my stomach, down to my belly bottom, down to my mid part on to the inside of my leg, and down to my feet. I laid there crying because I had found the love of my life. He was making love to me with his mouth and then he began to make love to me. The first time we did it, I just cried and held him as he made hot, passionate love to me. He held me right. He took his time with me and made love not only to my body, but also my heart and mind. I was in love. It didn't stop. We had sex two more times in my bed. Then we went and got in the tub and made love while the shower was going. I felt like I was in a movie making love like that. It was completed. He had my mind, my heart and he had me. And to top it all off, he wanted a baby. That was all I needed to hear. So as time went on, we would hang out at school. Everybody knew I was his and he was mine. We were in love; we were the couple of the year. Everything was good. I was on cloud nine. We had sex every day. On the weekends he would wait until my mom left to come to my house or I would wait until my mom left to go to work and call him to come get me, Luke and I would go back to his house where he ,his mom, and his sister stayed. His mom and I got along real well. I loved Ms. White and Ms. White loved me. I was happy. She would ask about me all the time when she didn't see me. She would let me know if Luke was acting out at home or in school and tell me to talk to him. I would leave home in the morning like I was going to the bus stop and I would walk over to his house and make love to him before school. His mom would tell me to go on in his room, you're family. I know what you all doing. I want my son to be happy. I was in heaven. Some days he couldn't come over because he had to work. I would make sure I got sex from him that morning because I knew I wouldn't see him after school. His dad would come get him and take him to work. His dad was in love with me too. I was his daughter. He would tell Luke, this is the one I want you to marry. We laughed and talked about it. I was just 15 years old. Luke was 16 years old, but he looked like he was about 18 or 19. So time went on and I wasn't having a period. I told him I didn't have a period. He got happy and said you might be pregnant. We got happy because we both wanted a child. He was working and buying me what I wanted. Me and my mom were getting into a lot. She was going to throw my stuff away because my grades began to drop from A's and B's to D's and F's. I didn't care because I knew it was because I was in honor classes. I was scared to tell the teacher I was in special needs classes because I didn't want Luke to break up with me. I didn't say anything. I'm failing, my period still has not come and my body is changing. I don't know what's wrong. I did know I was in love and about to have a baby with the man I loved. At least that's what I thought. One day I went to school and Luke and I told my teacher what was wrong. She took me to the clinic at the school and gave me a pregnancy test. The test came back positive. I was happy but scared. The nurse asked me if my mother knew. I told her no and I didn't want her to know because she would make me get rid of my baby. My mother had always told me if I got pregnant she would take me to the doctor and make them get rid of my baby. The nurse said, first of all, you need to see a doctor and she can't make you get rid of your baby if you don't want to. Second, if you are about three months they won't do it. She asked me when was my last period. I told her and she said you could be about four weeks or five. But she could not say anything to my mother because that was my right. Later that day at lunch, me and Leah were sitting there and I was sad because even though Luke said he wanted a baby, I was scared he would leave me. When he came over, he hugged me and kissed me and said what's up baby why you look so sad. Did you and your mother get into it or something. I looked at him, took his hand and walked off with him. I began to cry as he held me and asked me what was wrong I said I need to know if you really love me. He said, yes baby, what's wrong I told him the nurse gave me a test and it came back that I was pregnant. He began jumping up and down yelling I'm a daddy. So that day we were just happy. After school he came over we talked I told him I can't tell my mom yet because she will make me get rid of my baby. He said ok, I will tell my mom when you tell your mom. I said that's cool. He said I've got to tell my dad, he will be happy I said no he will tell your mother. Luke said no he won't, We were happy. We began to make love again on a daily basis. Time went on he was tell everybody months and months went by we really was the couple. So two months passed and school was getting ready to be out for the summer. so my mom next door kids told they mom I was with child and one day why we were at school Rita's mom, Ms. Nikki, told my mom she had heard I was with child. When I got home and walked through the door, my mom ran up on me and grabbed me and started hitting me and saying, you with child now. I cried and said no. She said that's what Rita told her mother. I was mad and hot and said people needed to mind their own business. That night Luke came to the house and I told him my mom knew about the baby because Rita told her mother. He said it was ok because he told his mother and if my mother put me out, I could stay with him. I was thinking about going to stay with my dad. His mom said she wanted a grandchild, but come to find out, she was just talking. But she wasn't nasty to me. That night I wrote my mother a note telling her I was with child and I had taken a test at school and it came back to positive. I told her the Luke's name and how he had been coming over while she was at work. I told her I would leave for school and go to his house before school and how I loved him. Before I went to school the next day, I put the note on the TV so she could read it. When I got out of school, my mom was at work and the note was gone. I was scared because I knew it was all over for me. My mother was going to kill me. The phone rang and I answered it. It was my mom. She began to go off on me and asked me all kind of questions. She told me not to go to bed because she was going to beat me. I waited for her that night. I was scared. I knew I was going to be beat, but when she got home she just yelled and slapped me a few times and talked about me like a dog. I went to school the next day and told Luke. He hugged and kissed me and told me everything would be ok. We would go stay with his dad if my mother put me out. So when I got home, my mother was off work. I didn't know it. As we were leaving to go to the doctor, Luke was walking up on the side walk. I looked at him and shook my head letting him know it wasn't going to work today. Once we got to the doctor, my mom was mad and she wanted blood work. While we waited for the blood work, the nurse took us in a room to talk to us. The labs came back and I wasn't pregnant. I cried and said the one at school said I was. My blood work came back and showed I had ovarian cancer, which sometimes shows up in pee as a pregnancy. After we left the doctor, my mom wanted me to take her to Luke's house. I did because I was scared. She was talking about putting him in jail. I prayed to God that he would not be there. When we got to Luke's house, no one was there but his sister. She got ready to say he went to work, but I looked at her with water in my eyes and shook my head. She didn't say anything. I went to school and I did see him at all that morning to let him know what was going on. My mom came to the school to get paperwork and to get me out of school. I thought she was taking me to the doctor but she had a rental car with all my stuff packed up. She took me back to Mobile never to see Luke again.

Chapter 9
Why do I keep ending up here?

We were driving on I-75 North. I was mad and crying because my mother had taken me out of school to bring me back to live with my grandmother. She didn't let me tell Leah bye. She didn't let me tell the one person who cared deeply about me bye. I didn't get to tell him I wasn't with child or what was wrong with me. So now I really hated my mother. She was yelling and hitting me as she drove to Mobile. I wished we would just fall over in the water and die. She didn't want me to be happy, so now I just wanted to die. The doctor said I had cancer and needed more tests run so they could begin me. I just wanted to die. I wished I could just go away from this family I didn't want to be in this family. I was at granny's house as my granny went off on me and called me all kind of names. I was mad and hated her. I didn't want to there with them. They were the reason I was the way I was. If she wasn't out at the bingo hall, I wouldn't have gotten raped and beat by my cousins. I hated my cousins and didn't want anything to do with them. I wanted to kill them. I wanted to cause everyone in the house hell now that I had nothing to live for. If God were to come and take me, I would have been happy. If I went to hell it couldn't be as bad as being here on earth. My mother, granny and my auntie were talking about the cancer. I didn't care because I felt as if I'd lost everything anyway. Before my mother left she came to tell me bye. I just looked at her and didn't say anything. She said, oh you supposed to be mad. I still didn't say anything to her. As she left, I cried like a baby because she was really leaving me. I had to stay and wouldn't be back for school or anything. When Granny left I got on the phone to call Luke. He was not at home so I told his sister I was in Mobile at my granny's house and I would call him back later. I called Leah and told her where I was. I told her I was back at my granny's house and I would be down there for the summer. I asked her to please tell Luke so he would know. I also told her about my mother. She asked me about the baby, but I just said we were find because I wanted to be the one to tell Luke what was going on. I also didn't want him to know I had cancer just in case my mom let me come back to Miami for school. The next day when granny left I called Luke and told him most of everything. I told him I was at my granny's house for the summer, but I would be back for school. I cried because I knew I wasn't coming back but kept hope that my mother would come back and get me. I told him I lost the baby because my mother made me get rid of the baby. I lied and told him it was a boy. I didn't want him to know it wasn't a baby; it was cancer. I talked to him for about two weeks before my granny got her phone bill. Her phone bill was four hundred dollars. She asked whose number it was. I lied and said I don't know, but granny called and found out it was Luke and told my mother. I got beat and I was told never to call him again. Still at this time I was going to the doctor to have more tests run on me to see what stage my cancer was in. so I had ovarian cancer and they weren't giving me long to live. I felt fine but they said Ms. Godwin, she is in her last stages and all we can do is give her treatments so she won't be in pain. I remember my dad's sister and how she had cancer and how when she started taking medicine she got real sick. The doctor told my grandmother not only did I need treatments, but I would never have kids. So now my mother had taken me form Luke, I had cancer and on top of it all, I wouldn't have kids. My life was a mess all over again. I just wanted to die. When I got home, I went upstairs. My granny told my mom and she acted as if she didn't care. She didn't even talk to me. My grandmother was talking about me like a dog saying she was not going to bother with me and this mess as she called it. I sat upstairs in the bathroom crying and once again tried to kill myself. I took five headache pills thinking that would kill me. They did nothing but made me go to sleep. When I woke up I realized I was still here on earth and I began crying again. My Aunt Deidre came upstairs crying and hugging me and talking to me about cancer. I looked at her and asked her why my mom took me away from the only person who ever loved me and cared about me. As she sat there with me crying and holding me and rocking me as she said, I don't know baby but it will be ok. So time went on, the doctor would call and send papers in the mail for me to be treated. I would not go back to the doctor. My aunt and my granny got mad at me for not going. My aunt beat me in my back and yelled at me to go because she didn't want me to die. Granny said leave her alone that her dumb (a**). I don't care. I looked at both of them and I yelled, "I want to die because no one loves me and my mother don't care about me. The person who does love me, yawl took me from him." My granny cursed me out and said, "Well die. It don't make me a bit of difference. Do what you feel." Then she got up and left and went to bingo. I was left at home with my auntie and my cousins. It didn't matter anymore if they raped me or not because I wanted to die. They didn't touch me because they thought they could get cancer if they had sex with me. So now I was rejected my them too. I was there in a world all by myself. I was mad at God. Why did he let me get beat? Why did he let me get raped? Why did he let my mother take me away from Luke? Why did he let me get cancer? What did I do that was so bad? What? I went back in the room and got my clothes out to get ready for church. I needed to know what did I do to deserve this. I got ready and went to church with the lady across the street, Ms. Jackson. At church the preacher began talking and saying God wants to heal you. God wants to heal your pain. He wants to heal your body. I went to the altar crying and telling the Lord I was sorry, please help me. I didn't want to die. I just wanted someone to love me .I wanted Luke back. Lord, please send Luke back. Lord, please give me a baby. I went back home. I felt better, but I was still mad at my mother and at my family. I hated them all. I was doing any and everything to make them mad so my mother could send me back to Miami. Even if I went back to my dad, I would be fine because I was older and could get to Mobile. One of my sisters stayed in Miami. I could tell my sister I wanted to stay with her and my dad would have said yes. But the more I acted up, the more I got beat by my uncles, cousin Benson, my granny. I didn't care. School was back in. I was back in the 9th grade because I didn't pass in Miami. But now I was back in Mobile in the right classes not the honor classes. I started to do right. I still hated everyone in my family. I would just do me until the Lord called me home from the cancer that I thought I had. I lied. I fought at school. I started to hang out with my auntie, my cousin Benson and his woman. My cousin Cedi was in jail so it was just me, Benson, my auntie and her boys who were about 10 and 11. Granny still went to bingo every day. My auntie and my uncles still went around the corner to sell drugs. My cousin sold drugs. I was at home cooking and cleaning and holding the drug money. If any one came by while they were gone, I was to sell drugs to the crack heads. My cousin's best friend, Larry, would come to the house. and I liked him. We were having sex when no one was there. He held me and made love to me like Luke used to. I would cry and he would think he was hurting me. I cried because he was made love to me like Luke used to and I missed Luke. I wanted to see him but I knew I was not going back to Miami. . I didn't have a phone number or address for Luke. I couldn't find him. I couldn't call Leah anymore either because her number had changed. I had to imagine that Larry was Luke. I made love to Larry as if he were Luke and I began falling for Larry. But I knew I couldn't be with him like that because he was like member of the family. Also, my family would have had him put in jail because I was just 16 and he was 26 or 29. We would just do it when we could. My hate demon was stronger. My sex demon was stronger. My lying demon was stronger. I sold drugs and I was at home taking care of kids that were not mine. I had to cook in a hot house and clean up after people like I was the maid. I got tired of it and so I would not have to cook and clean up and watch other people's kids, I got a job at Bell Tosca working at night. Thank God. I was out of that hell hole and made my own money. I didn't depend on anyone and didn't care what happened now because I made my own money. I didn't have to cook or eat at granny's because I could eat at work all day for free. My grandmother hated my job in a way because I always had to work. Even when I did not have to work, I called in so to see if they needed help. As some people would have called me being grown, I called it getting away from life. So as time went on, I began talking to all different kids back to back-- drug dealers, want to be thugs, my cousin's friend. I talked to and wrote guys that were locked up with my cousin Cedi. When Cedi called I would get to talk to them. Some worked outside the jail and could send money home. My cousin would act like he was sending me a note home from him, but it would be from the guy I was talking to. Every guy I talked to was abusive or just wanted one thing from me. They would get caught lying or cheating on me. I got tired of being used and started playing the field Until one day when I meet Edwin Smith. Edwin was 6'1", real light skinned with long, pretty hair that he kept braided up. He worked at King Chicken. I met him when I was in the 10th grade and worked at Bell Tosca. I was not supposed to be talking to boys, at least that was what my granny, my uncles and my cousin Benson said. They said if they caught a boy in my face, they were going to beat me and the boy. I didn't care what they said. No one loved me. The one who said he loved me did not because he let my mom take me away and did not try to stop it or come look for me. I thought, what the hell I will be 18 in a minute. So I met this guy. He was so soft, he would do anything I asked him to do so I would tell my grandmother I was working late and that my boss lady would bring me home. She said ok. She didn't care. If I were a grandson they would probably have cared. I would get off at one in the morning and I would make him get a room. I would take a bath, lay up with him and be with him until three in the morning. Granny would believe it because she knew we closed at 12 and we had to stay and clean up. Some nights I was supposed to get off at ten. I would call my granny and tell her my boss lady was bringing me home so I could be with him at a hotel or at his mother's house, which by the way they didn't like me at all. I found that out real soon. I did not like them either. I just wanted her son and what her son could do for me. So as time went on, we were dating and we were going to get married and all this stuff I didn't really want because I was hoping my mother would come and get me so I could go home to Luke. Time went on, I was in school but got kicked out because my cousin Benson's girlfriend was talking about him because they had broken up. I hooked my cousin up with one of my friends and his ex-girlfriend got mad and started talking about me and telling people what she was going to do to me. She had taken nasty photos of herself for my cousin, so I took the photos to school and made copies and put them up all around the school and gave them to the football team and the weight team. I had to stop working so I could go to EJC Adult High School so I could graduate. I had to go to school in the morning and at night so I could graduate on time or before time. I went to school Monday thru Thursday from 9 am until 7pm. It hurt, but I got it done. I was still with Edwin. He wanted to go in the army. I didn't want him to go so I lied and told him I was pregnant. If he went, I would be hurt and alone. He wanted to get married, but I didn't. By this time, my granny and everybody knew I was with him. Granny beat me because she knew about him. My cousin beat me. The only one who was happy for me was my auntie. I told her everything and she knew what I was going through. My auntie was gay and didn't know how to tell my granny, so she would lie for me and I would lie for her. Finally, one day my auntie told my granny she was gay. Granny told her she had to get out. My auntie was gone and she took her boys. My cousin didn't care anymore about what I did because he had his own thing going on. He didn't care that my uncle was in jail, I did what I wanted. Every now and then my uncle Mike would come by and try to tell me what to do and hit me. My mother didn't care. She had her life. She told my granny to put me in an all-girls school. It would not have mattered. The sex demon I had did not care if it was hungry, he was going to feed. It didn't matter if it were a boy or girl, My granny told my mother that I was still going to do I wanted, so she wasn't going to put me in an all-girls school to be gay like my auntie. I wanted to be with Edwin so I ran away from home. I waited until my grandmother went to bingo. I told Edwin to come get me, I was pregnant and my grandmother was kicking me out and I have nowhere to go. He told his mother and she allowed me to stay because Edwin went off on her about me and she didn't want to lose her son. Edwin had made up his mind that he was going in the army. I was mad but while he was gone, I stayed with his mom. I drove him to Tallassee to his cousin's house. That night we made love one more time before he left. I knew I was not with child but I tried hard to get pregnant by him. It didn't happen. When I got back home with his mom, they acted funny with me. I began leaving and staying gone all day like I was going to school. Or I would stay in the room just crying because it wasn't supposed to be like this. I was supposed to be in Miami with my mom and with Luke. Edwin's mother Rachel and I were getting into it. I would go to church with her to try to get her to like me. She did not try to meet me half way and her boyfriend Keith would fill her head up with all this stuff but all along he wanted me and I was not trying to get with him. We went to see Edwin at boot camp because he was getting ready to graduate and come home. When we got there his mother told him all this stuff about me and we got into a big fight. We had sex and that was the end of it, but as the weekend went on his mother made things worse. We went back to the room and I told him when I got home I would be leaving his mother's house. He got mad. When we got back I started packing and took my stuff to my auntie's house. I stayed with this person and that person because my auntie's girlfriend did not want me there.

Chapter 10

Life as a young adult

Well here I am at 18 years old, working at Hams Chicken in Foley, Alabama. I was making good money and had just moved into the Home Ville Apartments. They were nice one bedroom apartments with a nice size living room, a big bed room, and a nice size kitchen with a back door that lead to the outside or to the back door of someone else's apartment. I moved upstairs in apt. A. did I tell you will pool side "hum" a girl dreams no man no kids making money still the demons are still there only if I had someone to come home. Not worrying about my family don't care if they found me or not Benson and my auntie knew where I was but it was just like they did not know because they didn't come over. (Love Right, Hum). So here I am working all the time. I was not at home a lot because of the way I worked. And when I was at home, I was sleep so I could get ready for work. I didn't have time to meet the people that were around me. This week I was off work because I had vacation time. I was sitting outside on the porch just enjoying the outside and looking at all the little kids in the pool with their parents. As I started seeing some of my neighbors, they would speak and say so I was lucky that I moved upstairs. I smile and wondered what they meant. What did they know that I didn't. On the bottom were two couples that were married. I was the single woman in apartment A and next to me was a single man, but I had never seen him. I was like whatever because I was not looking for any one because I was tired of people saying they love me and all the while they were beating me or raping me or leaving me. So I didn't care and when it came to sex I just go and get one of the men I had already been with and we would do what we do and he would leave. So as I sat there on my porch, a gray and purple truck pulled up. I waited to see who got out because I had met just about everybody that stayed on the side where I stayed. So as I sat there this tall, 6'1, dark skin, nicely built ,handsome, well-dressed man got out of his truck. As I sat there looking at him get out his truck, I said to myself who is that and I hope and pray that he is my next door neighbor. As he walked up on the sidewalk, I looked at him as he looked at me with a smile as if he were saying is this who stays next to me. As he walked up stairs I looked at him and gave him a half of a smile and said hi. He looked at me and said hi with a smile and said so you are the new person. I responded by saying, "yes." I laughed as he shook my hand. I looked at him and I wanted to say you can put those hands all over me. He said my name is Ricky. I said nice to meet you, my name is Kashia. He said welcome Kashia, if you every need something I am here. I knew you just moved in and I know you will need to use the phone and things so that fine. As I sat there saying to myself, yes I need something, you all over my body. But I just smiled and said thanks. So he opened his door as I sat there thinking ok he's not into me, so I need to stay my distance. I got up and got ready to go inside my house. When I stood up, I had on this sun dress on that made my chest sit up. My hair was right; I was looking RIGHT. So as he came back outside and said you leaving I said yes but if you're coming back out I will stay out. I said well I would invite you in, but I do not have anything for you to sit on. We laughed and he asked if he could see my place. I said yes there is nothing in it but my bed and clothes and my bathroom is fixed up. So he said ok I understand. And then he said your husband or your boyfriend is not going to get me. I looked at him because I knew where he was going with this. He was trying to find out if I had someone. Then he said, oh your place looks like mine. Looking at all your photos, I tell you don't have kids neither. I laughed and said you don't have to beat around the bush. Just ask. No I don't have a man, I have friends that I get with every now and then. And I don't have kids because I have not found that one. So he smiled and said well that's good what do you do, I said I'm a manager at Ham Chicken in Foley. So he said ok that's why I never see you until today. And I said yes, I'm on vacation this week. So he began to look around some more and then I said well what do you do. He said well in the mornings I go to school. I said wow what do you major in? He said accounting. I said ok, and then he said, I work at night at Store Depot. I said ok, it sounds like your day is very busy he said yes and smiled and said but I will make time for you. I smiled, looked at him and made love to him with my eyes as he made love to me with his eyes. So I said well ok well we will see. So so he said do you work out? By looking at your body you look like you work out. I said no. Do you? He said yes I'm a member at Mold's Gym. I said well, I don't work out, but I would love to work out with you. He laughed as he said I work out at a fast pace. I said ok if it's too much I know how to stop. So we talked a little more. Then he said, well I got to go and get ready for work. As I looked at him and said ok well I'm here now so you are welcome any time. That was for him to come and have sex with me that night because my body was over heated for him. So now I know who my neighbor is and why they were saying I'm the lucky one. Hmm. Lucky was right. So now I know what time he goes to school and gets out and I also know what time he goes to work and gets off. So that whole week I was off, I would wait until ten minutes before he got out of school to go sit on my porch, or I would wait to hear him pull up and open my blinds so he could see me or I would see him so I could speak to him or so he would say something to me. So now it's time for me to go to work. I don't see him as much. For about two weeks we would pass each other. I would be leaving and he would be just coming in from school so it was like hi how are you today and he would say I would love to have some of that chicken from your job. I would laugh and say I will see, it depends on how our night is. So on this one week, I was working nights and school was out for college students so we would see each other for like that whole week in the morning. So we began to work out that week and as we worked out he was like my little coach. As he was coaching me, we are flirting. This week every day we worked out we would go get in the pool so we would not hurt the next day, or so I would not be hurting because he went to the gym every morning before school. So this day we worked out and it was so much flirting going on that day we could have had sex right there on the gym floor. We walked back to the house from the gym because it was right around the corner from our apartments. He was like are you getting in the pool and I said sure. I go home and change out of my gym clothes and take all my rings off. I came back out with a bathing suit on and a shirt that came right to my thighs. He walked out with just some shorts and no shirt on. We looked at each other as if both of our minds was on sex that day. We look at each other and made little complements to each other. As we got in the pool, we began talking about life and what we like and don't like. We found out that we had so much in common. So after we got out the pool he said would you like to come get lunch with me I 'm cooking. I looked at him and said do you know how to cook. He replied of course and I said sure why not, let me go and take a bath and put on some clothes. He said you don't have to be all dressed up to come eat. I want to see you with no make-up on, no cute little clothes or heels on. I laughed and said that's how I do, but I will dress down because after I get done eating, I'm going to sleep. So I went and changed clothes and came back over. I took my nails and tapped softly across his door. He opened it and said I like that, that's going to be our knock for each other's door. I said ok. As I came in his house looked just a bachelor pad. The big bean bag was in the living room where he sit and lay with his TV and all his CDs and his DVDs his exercise equipment his house nice and clean. As we sat at his table eating and looking into each other's eyes and making love with our eyes, my body is getting heated and ready for him to make a move on me. So as we get done eating we go lay down on the big bean bag. As I lay in his arms watching TV, he takes his big soft hands and rubs on my legs as I began to fall asleep. He began to kiss my ear and my neck while holding me. As he kisses me, I play like I am sleep, but all the while I love it. As I turn over, he looks at me with those big pretty brown eyes and says do you want me to stop. I look at him and pull him closer to me and began to kiss him back. While I undressed him, he smiled and turned on the jazz CD. He began to undress me and kiss me all over and make love to me. As I lay there crying because the more he makes love to me the more I think about how Luke used to make me feel when he made love to me. And I did not know what to do. Because here it was, I gave my heart to Luke and my mother took me away. Now I'm here again with this man and I didn't know how this was going to work out. I was scared, lonely, and wanted my man back and could not have him. Thinking to myself is this love that I'm feeling or does it just feel good at the moment. That day Ricky made love to my ear, to my neck, to my mouth, to mind and to my body. He tried to make love to my heart but I would not let him because my heart was for one man and one man only, and that was Luke. As he stopped and looked at me, I asked him what's wrong. He said nothing, I just want to look at you. You are so beautiful. As I smiled at him and pulled him closer to me, we made hot, mad, passionate love to the Jazz CD. So that night he had to go to work and I went home and just cried because this man had made hot, passionate love to me like I wanted him to. He looked good. He had a good heart. He was a great listener. Everything about him was good and I was scared to give him my heart because I didn't want to be hurt anymore by a man or by family. So as the days went by I avoided Ricky because I had to get my head together and because he was trying to go someplace I was not ready for, and that was my heart. So that week he would knock on my door and I would not answer. I would not go to his house. And when I got off work, I would not knock on his door or call him. So that week had gone by and as he came home I was sitting in the living room watching TV and he knocked on my door. I sat there and he knocked again. As I opened the door he looked at me and said are you mad at me. I said no why would I be? He said I have been knocking on your door and you don't answer, you don't call and you don't come over. Did I do something wrong? Is this about last week? I stood there wanting to cry and tell him how I felt, but I said it's about last week but you did not do anything wrong. I just need time to get my head together. I will get with you in a day or two. As he looked at me as if he had messed up or something, I closed my door and cried with my back against the door. I cried because he had everything I wanted and needed. He just was not the person I wanted. I said to myself why can't he be Luke? Why did this have to happen to me? What did I do to get this? So I went and laid across my bed and began writing letters to Ricky tell him what was wrong and how I felt. So the next few days passed by. I was on my to work when I put the letter on his door. When I returned home, Ricky's door opened. I looked, but kept on going in my house and put my things on the counter. He walked over and grabbed me from behind, hugged me and said I need you to know I'm not here to hurt you. I'm here for you and I do understand how you feel. I didn't know that's how you felt. I looked in his eyes, making love with my eyes, and said well now you know. I understand if this is too much for you. He smiled and picked me up and began kissing me. I said wait I just got off work and I need to take a shower. I brought food home if you have not eaten. He said that's cool, go take a bath and lock up and come to my place and stay the night with me. That was right up my alley because I wanted and I needed that somebody to lay next to and wake up next to. But I was still cautious because I knew we were not a couple; we were just friends. So I got done with my bath, locked up and went to his house. I laid in his arms and made love to him all night. I was happy as I could be. I only wished it was Luke that was there. My sex demon was very happy because she was getting what she needed to make her stronger. As time went on we began acting like a couple, although we never said that we were a couple. We just did what lovers did-- cook for each other, laugh with each other talk to each other about life and what we wanted, made love to each other, and stayed the night at each other's house. It was great, but I was still doing me on the side. I had bills; he had bills and school and I did not ask him for anything because I felt he was doing enough just by being there when I needed him emotionally and sexually. By now have left Ham Chicken and I'm working at Blue County Hospital in housekeeping. I'm lying up with all these different men because I only have enough money to pay my rent, but I began to find a man, D-Nice, to pay my rent. But before he paid it I gave him sex. And the only time I would mess with him was around the first of the month so I could get my rent paid. Then I had a man, Pooh, who paid my light bill. But before he paid my light bill, I had to give him sex. I only called him in the second week of the month to get my lights paid. I had a man, Bobby, for my cable and phone bill. But before he paid I had to give him sex. On top of everything I still laying up with Ricky just because he was making love to my body like I needed. He was the only one that could do me like Luke did as far as when it came to sex and talking and acting like he cared. But as I was doing me, Ricky didn't know at first until after one night when me and him made love, the next day I had the light bill man over and Ricky knocked on my door. I didn't answer and I waited until I thought he was sleep and told the guy to go home. But Ricky was not sleep. He heard the guy leave and that night when he left Ricky called me and said I thought we had something and I was falling in love with you and this is how you do me. And I knew it was over, so I just said look I told you that I have guy friends I talk to. We began yelling and I said Ricky I'm sorry but I didn't know we were a couple. You never said we were. We hung up that night and did not talk to each other for about a week or two. I was upset with myself because here I am got someone who wanted to be with me and I messed up by [prostituting my body to get my bills paid. I had lost out again. Why did this keep happening to me? What did I do to have things end up like this? So here I am all alone with no one to talk to. Ricky was not there to make love to me and hold me to. I just shut up and didn't say anything to anyone. I just went to work. When I did see Ricky I said hi and kept going. He looked at me like he wanted to say something, but didn't. Time went on and he began talking to this girl in his class. He would bring her back to his house and he would say that was his study buddy but I wasn't dumb because I would hear the same Jazz music or R&B songs he would play with me. I knew I had lost him for real now. So I began just doing me, going out, not caring about anything or anyone. I would still go to work and just pay my rent. My lights got cut off for about two and a half months. I didn't say anything to Ricky because I was mad at myself and I was mad at him for talking to that other woman. But one day in came over and he said he wanted to talk. We began to talk (this was in the morning so he did know that the lights were off until that night because he wanted to stay the night with me). When I opened my door he asked me if he could stay the night. I said something is wrong with my fuel box as he went to get his stuff to try to fix it I told him don't worry about it, I will get it done in the morning. So he said well will you come stay the night with me. And I said so are we done fighting? He smiled and said man yes and kissed me. But we were still not together. We were just friends having sex. The the sex had changed. We would just do it. There was no love making, no music. We would just have sex, eat, and go our own way. He still had his friend and I was still working and staying in my cold house with no lights. So that next week as soon as it got hot I got a roommate, one of my home girls that I sold drugs to. She was on drugs but not that bad.

She had a car and a good job working down town. She began moving in her stuff and went and got herself a bed. My room was big enough to put two full sized beds in it, so she moved in. She would work in the morning and I would work in the evening until eleven. Ricky and I would still do our thing. This lasted about six months when I called my cousin at home and we started talking, I told her I trying to found a cheaper place to stay. She said she had a town house and no one was there but her and her my son who slept with her. I could have his room if I gave her two hundred dollars until I got on my feet and found something. I said ok and I told the girl that was my roommate if she wanted to stay, she could but I going to take my name off the lease because I was moving in with my cousin.

She said ok no she would go back where she was. I told Ricky I was leaving and moving with my cousin. He asked why and I told him I couldn't afford the apartment anymore. He was like ok. The whole week we stayed together and had sex. The last night I left, he went over to the apartment and went to sleep one last time but he laid by himself because I left and went to stay with my cousin. A few days went by and he called me to come over and have sex and I did because I needed to feed that demon. Days went by and I stopped over Ricky's place before I called. He answered the door and when he saw it was me his eyes got big. A woman was in the bathroom getting herself together. I looked at her and I looked at him and said I'm sorry didn't know she was over here. I turned to walk down the stairs and looked back at him saying good bye and never saw him again.

Chapter 11

Troubled Times

I was with my cousin Marta and her son Derek. Things were good, no bills, no man, still no kids. But you would think my life would be good. (YEA RIGHT). I was with Marta and her son. Marta is like a white girl in a black girl's body. She is real smart and she to works at Blue County Hospital in the lab with blood and stuff. She likes nice things. Like me, she loves to dress and look good and keep herself up. She is married but she her and her husband are separated because he did drugs and he beat her. So she knew all about getting beat and being done wrong. But the way she acted you would have thought she was married to a doctor or a lawyer or something. I didn't care about all of that because I had been around so many people, white, black, and mixed and knew how to act around them. So things were good. We laughed. We went shopping. We went out to eat.   I would tell her about the guys I went with and some of the stuff that happened to me with some of my family. I knew what to tell her and what not to tell her because she could not hold water. I told her about the guys I was with and as we talked she began to tell me about her husband and some guy she was talking to. She would tell me how she got them and how she got them to do what she wanted them to do. I looked at her and I was like whatever. Then she took me to her room and her closet and she pulled out all kind of candles and they had all different ladies on them. She had paper with stuff written on the paper. She said it was white magic and she began teaching me how to do white magic not knowing that was the devils work. I knew about voodoo because when I stayed with my dad. my uncle's girlfriend put it on him. They had to pay all this money for a voodoo doctor to come get it off him. But white magic, I didn't know what that was about. My cousin told me it was good and it wouldn't hurt me. I began going with her and learned how to get a guys hair and under clothes and burning candles. I would reading all this stuff three times a day when I woke up and before I went to bed. I was doing everything she told me. I was just doing it and everything I was doing and saying, was happening. I was loving this and got deep in doing it. So now I had a lying demon, a sex demon, a hate demon, a depressed demon, and a proud demon. And I'm working in voodoo. I was all messed up. I didn't care because it was all about me. I could not have what I wanted, so I got what I needed. I know some might think why didn't I try to go or have Luke found with the voodoo. Because as I got deep in it, my cousin told me if the person I do it on doesn't believe in voodoo it won't work. Or if they don't do what I say it will hurt them and sometimes kill them. I was not trying to hurt Luke or kill him, so I left him alone and just used it on people or things I didn't care about. So for about six months things were good. I went to work and came home. Me and Marta worked the 3 to 11 shift, so we were at work together and home together. We did everything together. If she had a friend over. that friend brought a friend with him. She would leave her son at her mother's house that night. She was in her room doing her, and I was doing me. Things were great. We got along real good. I got paid and I gave Marta her money. So about the end of the seventh month, I went to work and this guy named Black worked in the kitchen at the hospital. We became best friends. I didn't see him as someone I would talk to. He was fine, real crazy, and he was a true thug. I was like ok, just friends. He had a guy he hung out with, Carlos. Carlos was a Latino and just what I wanted. When he come up on the job, I would ask Black who is your friend. What's up? Does he date black girls? Black said he's one of us. I was asking about Carlos and if he wanted to talk to me. I didn't know it, but Black would play and mess with me, but I just saw him as a friend. So one day Carlos brought Black to work. I was outside and spoke to Carlos because I wanted him, not as a boyfriend but someone to have sex with on the regular. I wanted a baby by him because I wanted a baby so badly. I didn't care what the doctor said. I didn't feel sick and I was not hurting, so I wanted to try to see if I could get pregnant. But, that day Black said my home girl said hi and he smiled and turned down his music and said (Hey Mommy). As I thought that was so sexy so I smiled wanting him then. Black went inside and we began talking. I gave him my phone number and told him to call me. So when I went back in Black said that man got a girl and she just had a baby. I looked up at him saying so, I just want sex from him. I don't want him like that. Black looked at me and gave me this half way smile like he wanted to say something but he did not. So weeks went on and me and Carlos was talking on the phone. Then he said the magic words, CAN I COME OVER. I said yes. I knew it was on, so I told Black your boy's coming over. And he said, are you going to give him some. I looked at him and said you know it. So he said be careful. I asked him what that meant. He replied that man makes babies. I looked and said really. I smiled and said I will be ok. So that day me and my cousin were off. Carlos came over and I let him meet my cousin. That's when the spirit of jealously hit the house; he was a big demon. So as my cousin went in her room and got on the phone with her friend, me and Carlos were in my room doing us. After we began he said wait and pulled out this condom and put it on. I looked at him and said to myself this not going to work. We did the do. It only lasted for about four minutes. I looked at him and said my cousin is waiting on me, we're about to go so I will holler back later and I sent him back home to his woman. And I went and got myself cleaned up. I went and lay across my cousin's bed and talked about him. My sex demon was so upset because it was hungry and what I had given it did not please it at all. So he and Marta laughed and she acted if everything was good, but it was not. I called Black and told him his friend was whack. I don't know how he got kids because he ain't working with nothing. We laughed. I said what are you doing? He said nothing. So I said, where do you stay. He said in the Moorings. I was like for real, you stay right around the corner from me. He was like for real. So I told him where I stayed and I told him to come over. I hung up the phone with him. Me and my cousin talked and I told her he was going to come over. She was like ok, but she was like real funny acting with me. She told her son to come in the room with her. I told her he could come in the room with me. Black was just my buddy. She looked at me crazy. And when Black came over, we were just chilling and her son came in the room where we were played with Black. We were cutting up all night. I showed him a book of my home girl and was trying to hook him up. He was like that's my cousin. I was like oh my bad. I had never seen him, but I knew all his people and had dated one of her cousins. We went back in the room and play wrestled. It turned into more than just playing. So as we played he got on top of me and held my arms down to the bed. He looked at me. I laid there and looked as he began to tell me how he wanted to be with me and how he wanted me. I asked him why didn't he say this earlier. He said he tried but I was into his boy. As I looked at him and said you do know I had sex with your boy. He said yes I know and I don't care about that. You said it did not mean nothing. I said it didn't, but how do you want to be with me and I had sex with Carlos. I said I don't want this to their friendship. He said, I don't care he know not to cross me because I will tell his baby mama. So I just looked at him and said well let me think about it. Because I was not looking for a boyfriend, I was happy doing me. So as he sat there looking at me, he got up and I hugged him. As I hugged him, I let him go and he sat on my bed looking in my eyes with that thug passion in his eyes. He leaned over and grabbed me by my neck and pulled me close to him and began kissing me. As he was kissing me, I began to undress him. We made love until late that night. As he left my cousin said, I thought it wasn't like that with you and him. She said doesn't he know you did it with his boy? I sat there and said yes he knows and he doesn't care. She looked at me as if she wanted to call me a (w***). So things were good. We began to be a couple. We had sex all the time, every day at home, or on our job. We would go up to the fifth floor or the sixth floor and we would go to rehab bathroom and just have sex. So later on in the month, Marta began to complain about small stuff, a plate being left in the sunk or why did Black have to come over every day, and if he was going to be staying the night, he needed to pay a bill. I knew what time it was, so I began to start looking for my own place because she was jealous of me. That spirit laid in that house and it began to attach itself to me. So the longer I stayed there, the more Marta began to make my stay a living (h***). I thought she was burning candles on me, so I began working white magic on her. Things began to

happen to her in a bad way. It went from us doing
everything together, to us not doing anything. She would
let things get cut off, so I would get out. She would go
stay with her mother and talk about me like a dog and go
and tell my family all this stuff about me. They would tell
her to kick me out, but she could not because I was
paying her two hundred dollars every two weeks. I was
also saving up money for that day when she would act
crazy. So one day I was at her house and she had just had
her landlord to come and change the locks on her doors.
When he opened the door he looked at me and said what
are you doing here, your cousin said you don't stay here
anymore. So I called her at work I should have known
something was wrong, because when I'm off, she's off.
But, this day she went to work. So I called her at work
and asked her what was going on. She said nothing and
began laughing. I told if she wanted me to move that was
all she had say. I was a big girl. She said, if that's what you
want to do, then you do that. I was just getting my doors
fixed because my mom has a key to my house and I don't
want anyone in my house when I'm not there. She did not
want me there, so I said ok and hung up my phone. So I
took off the next day and I went to Creek Tree
apartments and got a place of my own. I left the window
unlocked to my room at Marta's house because she didn't
give me a key. I said ok, I know how to fix this. Pay day
was that week and when I got paid I didn't give her any
money. The money I had saved up and the check I got, I
took to the Creek Tree and gave them my deposit and my
first month's rent. The next day I went to work and she
did to because she had started a new job working in the
morning. That night I worked the 11 pm to 7 am shift and
the guys that worked there knew me. I asked them to help
me move my stuff to my house that morning when we got

off. They did. I moved all my stuff to my house and I spent the day cleaning and fixing up my apartment. I was happy I had my own place again. When I left Marta's house I left a candle in the room I was in. It was burning. I didn't have her name written on anything. I left the candle on trying to burn down her house because I began to hate her. When she saw me at work, she said you could have told me you were leaving, I would have gotten you a house warming gift. She started laughing. I began doing dirty things to her like calling HRS on her so she could have her child taken away. I would go to her boss and complain on her. I would do any and every thing I could think of to get her in trouble. But little did I know she was doing things back to me and trying to get me fired. But it didn't work because I had already told the people at work what she had done and the people on her job didn't care for her because she thought she was better than everybody there. She would tell some of the people I worked with about some of my past. Me and Black began to fight a lot and he would stay out a lot with his friend and drink heavily and smoke weed. When he did stuff like that we would fight like cats and dogs. Our first Christmas together was real crazy. He would I get real drunk and start to fight. I would tell his mom, Ms. Pat. She would tell me leave Black alone he wasn't any good. His mother worked with us to and she would tell me to put him out and don't let him come back. His granddaddy and his grandmother, Mr. and Mrs. Williams, would tell me the same thing, but I didn't want to listen because I was in love (lust). I had gotten used to people telling me they loved me and then hurt me. I thought that was love me getting beat and having sex all the time. We were at work and he got a gift from one of the girls on the job. He was acting if they were together.

His mom said baby it's not anything. But I was not trying to hear that. So when I got home, I told him not to come to my house. We were done. He was not trying to hear that. We got into it bad and when we got done I called his mother and said your son is hitting me you need to come get him or he will be going to jail. That was the only way I could get him to leave. When he left I took a big clear trash bag and put all his clothes all his gifts that he had got from people on our job and the blanket his grandmother bought for us and put it in the bag. I had some bleach from work, that strong bleach that all it takes is a cap full to do the job. I poured the whole the container in his cloths, his work cloths and the gifts. I put the bag outside in the cold and called his mother and told her to come and get his stuff. She said I'm not because you are going to let him come back. I said ok that's what you think. You can come get it or it's going in the trash. So the next morning he and his granny came and got his stuff. As I looked out my window, sad and mad on the inside, but my outside was laughing because I messed up everything he had. My phone rang. I didn't pick up. Black kept calling. I didn't say anything, but when I got to work everybody knew what I had done. They began laughing and calling me crazy.

That stuck with me and I began to act as if I was crazy so the next man that came in my life would get something worse if he hurt me. Black's mother looked at me and laugh and said you bleached all my baby clothes. I said so. She said you didn't have to do him like that. I said I told you last night to come get his stuff. I walked off as he came behind me and grabbed me and asked why I did what I did. I looked at him and said if you don't get your hands off me you will lose your job next and go to jail. After that day I would see him in the hall, but we didn't say anything to each other. He looked at me and I would look at him with a crazy look, but deep inside I wanted him to come back home. But because that proud demon was there, I just kept on going on about my business. He quit Shorty and began talking to someone else. I didn't see him anymore and in the same week my cousin Marta got fired.

Chapter 12

My Back is Against the Wall

My birthday was right around the corner. I was about to be 20 years old. I had no man, I was lonely. I wanted somebody that I could come home to. I work, come home, and go to sleep. On my birthday I got off work and was getting ready to go get my hair done and my nails done for my birthday. I had just got done cleaning up my house. All I had to do was wash but I would do that when I came back from getting my hair and nails done. I just got my hair and nails done and was on my way back home. I entered my house, put my things down and went to go and get the dirty clothes so I could go to the washroom in my complex. As I walked to the washroom, I saw a big truck that said, "RENT TODAY." They looked like they were lost. I didn't stop, I kept on going. When I came back out the washroom and began to walk to my apartment, the truck pulled up with two fine brothers in the truck. The truck pulled up on the side of me. The light-skinned brother with the green eyes and good wavy black hair said, Excuse me sweetie, do you know where apartment 182 is?" I said, No, but I'm 162. So, you got to be close to it." I began to walk off to go back in my place and the guy said, "Excuse me sweetie. What's your name?" I gave him my name as I thought to myself yes, you can come over and be my man or my thing I do. I said, "Why?" He said, "Because my friend wants to get to know you." I said, "Oh, really? Why he so quiet? What's your friend's name?" The friend said, "My name is Steve." I said, "Hi Steve." I would have gone in my house and not said anything if I had known what the end was going to be. But, I was depressed and lonely and wanted a man to come home to and someone that would come home to me. I said, "My name is Kashia and as you know now I stay here in 162." Steve asked me for my phone number and I gave it to him. I told him if he called to call between three and eleven. He smiled and said, "Why? Your man be home at that time?" I said, "I live alone. I don't have any kids, but I do go to work at three until eleven at night." He said, Where do you work?" I said, "West Florida Hospital." He took out his cell phone and called my number to make sure the number I gave him was my number. I laughing and said, "Why would I give you a fake number? If I didn't want you to have my number, I wouldn't give it to you." He said, "I will call you tonight." I said, "Ok. I will be here. I'm off tonight." That night he called. We were talking and he asked if could he come over and spend some time with me for my birthday I said sure. I was lonely and I needed to feed my demon. He asked, "Have you eaten?" I said, "Earlier." He asked, "What can I bring you?" I wanted to say you, but I just played the shy road and said, "Nothing really. If you want to bring something, you can. It's up to you." He said, "Well, I have not eaten yet, so I will bring us something to eat." I said, "Ok." He said, Do you drink?" I said, "A little but only wine coolers." He said, "Ok, you don't drink." I said, "I do, but I don't know if you're ready for that person." He said, "What do you mean? You get crazy or something?" I said, "No that's when my inner woman gets higher." He said, "Oh really." I laughed and he said, "Well, I'll be over in about thirty to forty-five minutes." I got off the phone with him and went and took a shower. I put on my smell goods and a pair of short blue shorts, a blue and white see through shirt and a push up bra. I put baby oil all over me and with the new sew in wet and wavy hair, I looked like I belonged in the

Jet magazine. When I got done, I sat watching TV. Steve knocked on the door. I jumped up and ran to the door, but stood there until he knocked again. I opened the door. He stood there brown skin, 5'5", built, and dressed like an educated thug in nice clothes. His hat was pulled down to his eyes looking good and smelling good He looked at me and said, "(D***). That's what's up." I said, "What are you talking about?" He said, "You, looking like you looking." I smiled and said, "Come in." He brought Steak Out, some kind of drink named Mud Slide, a six-pack of wine coolers, and a card with money in it for my birthday. I tried to play hard and said, "You did not have to do this." But, as I stood there, I said to myself, "He is a keeper." I turned the TV off and turned the music on. We sat at on the couch eating and talking. I was sitting there trying to be cute and not eat. He said, "Man, you better eat and stop being cute. I want to know the real you." I smiled and said, "No, you don't. It's too early to know the real me." So we talked and drank and laughed. Then, we went in the kitchen and began cleaning up the dishes. I was like, wow he's cute and nice. He will feed me and bring gifts. Wow, he is really a keeper. He made one more drink for himself and asked if I wanted to try it. I had drank three wine coolers. I said, "Well, I will try it, it can't be that bad." Oh boy. I drank it. I already wanted him, but now I was feeling real good. I wanted him even more. I straddled his lap and kissed his lips, ear and neck. He took his hand and took off my shirt. We began to get really into it. I took his shirt off and began to undo his pants. He kissed me on my neck and left a hickey. We got more into it. I got up, grabbed him by his hand and led him into my bedroom. As we laid there, I asked him if he had a condom. He told me no he didn't wear them. I said that was ok because I couldn't have kids anyway. I wasn't worried about it. As we had sex, he began climaxing in me. I laid there thinking if only I could get pregnant, my life would be complete. I have a man here with all the right words and the right things and he's doing things I have never done in the bed. He has got to be the one. At least that's what I thought. Little did I know my life was about to get worse. He had just as many demons as I did. And the demons were strong and had been there for a long time. Steve stayed all night with me. About six o clock he got up and said good morning .I looked at him and wished could stay all day with me. We began having sex again. He said, "Well, I got to go. I got to go home and get dressed for work. I will call you later." Later that day he called and said, "What are you doing?" I said, "Getting ready for work. My supervisor is on her way to get me." He said, "You don't have a car?" I said, "No, but I will get one sooner or later," He said, "Do you take a break?" I said, "Yes, we go to lunch at six o'clock." He said, "Can I come eat with you?" I said, "I don't care. If you want to, that's fine." He asked, "What you want me to bring you?" I tried him and said, "Some hot wings from Wings To Go on Ninth Avenue." He said, "That's it?" I said, "Yep, they have drinks here that I get for free." So later that day he came to my job and met me in the lobby. When I got there he was standing there looking at me as if he just knew he had me. (I'm not going to lie, he did.) We went to the lunchroom and sat down. My co-workers came over and started being messy by saying Steve looked like Black. I said he didn't because there was no more Black. Steve looked at them and smiled as if he wanted to say the hell with Black there's a new Deputy in town. We ate then I said I had to go back to work. He said, "Ok sweetie." He hugged he and gave me a kiss and I walked him out to his car. I asked him if he wanted to come over to night when I get off. He said, "If you want me to." I said, "I'll leave that up to you. If you come bring your clothes so you can get dressed at my house and go to work." He said, "Tell your supervisor she don't have to bring you home tonight. I will come get you." I said, "Ok. That's cool, but you have to come to the ER because this side will be closed at ten." He said, "Ok." As I walked back in to go upstairs, I heard one of the girls say, "Humph, just drop one and get another like that." I turned around and said, "Baby, you got something you need to say to me?" I was always ready to fight. That demon stayed on ready. She looked at me she and said, "I'm just saying you messed up Black's stuff because you thought he was talking to someone up here and you all only been broke up for a few weeks. That's not right." I looked her and said, "Don't worry about my house. Stay in your house. Black ain't do right. I'm not going to have someone beating on me. Maybe where you from y'all do that. But not me. Since you're so worried about him, you go get him. Then I said, "Now if you got anything else you'd like to say to me, wait until we get off the job because I'm not going to lose my job over no foolishness. Holler at me when you get off." I walked off and went back to my post. The night came and we were in the clock out room getting ready to go home. I said, "Do you still need to holler at me?" She clocked out and walked off. I didn't know she had called Black and told him I was talking to someone else. Steve came and picked me up. We went home. While I took a shower, he laid across my bed and watched TV. When I got out, I put on purple, silk lingerie. I went in the room and he said, "What are you trying to do to me?" I smiled because I was trying to make him stay for good, not just spend the night. He went and took a bath. When he got of the tub, he came back in the room with just a towel on. I looked at him. My sex demon was getting heated. He laid in the bed. I looked at him and got on top of him. I kissed him on his neck, down to his chest, down to his belly button, down to his manhood, making love to him with my mouth. Once again we made love and did things I had never done or thought about doing. Later on that night Black came to my house drunk and loud and beat on my door yelling at the top of his voice, "Kashia, let me in. I know you have somebody else in there with you." I looked at Steve who said, "Do I need to handle this." I said, "No, he is drunk and he is a waste of time. Let him stay out there. Someone will call the police on him." Black said, "If you don't open the door, I will bust out your window to your house." I looked out the window and he had a bat. I said, "If you do, you will go to jail." He said, "Let me in." I said, "No, what do you want." He said, "I want to talk. I want to come back home." Steve got up, but I told him not to go out there and get in trouble. I told Black he needed to leave. It got quiet and Steve and I laid back down. Then Black came around the back of my apartment to my sliding glass door and some way opened it and got in. I heard my door open and jumped up and ran in the living room. I push him and told him to get out of my house. He said, "I want to know who is this nigga you with." I kept telling him to get out and I picked the phone up and called his mother. I told her, "Ms. Pat your son broke in my house. He's drunk and he won't leave. My friend is over here and I don't want your son to get hurt or go to jail. She said, "Baby, call the law." I told Black your mother told me to call the police on you. He said he didn't care. I told him to get out or tonight would be his last night. "You broke in my house and if I kill you I will get away with it." Black said, "Baby, please just come

outside and talk to me. Please." I said, "Ok, just get out.
He went out. I went back in the room and Steve looked at
me and said, Do I need to go?" I said, "No, for what?
We're not together anymore. Don't leave now, this fool
might hurt me or something." Steve sat up in the bed. I
put on a housecoat, went outside and sat on the stairs.
Black looked at me and said, "You sleeping with this
man?" He grabbed me by my arms and tried to kiss me . I
said, "Black move. It's nothing." He got mad and hoped
up and started walking towards my door. I ran and got in
front of the door and told him to move. He said, "You
love that nigga. What is he doing here? We just broke up a
few weeks ago." We got into it and he tried to open up
my robe to look and touch on me. I told him to move. It
didn't matter, I was not his anymore. He began crying and
saying he wanted to come back home, that he loved me
and missed me. As much I was turned on about it, I
began to push him away and said, "It's over." He looked
at me and hit the wall and said, "It's not over. If I can't
have you, no one else will have you. I'm going to blow
your boy up and his car." I said, "You need to leave." He
asked, "which one of these cars is his?" I would tell him,
so he ran up and grabbed me by my neck. He said, "Look
me in my face and tell me you don't want me no more." I
looked at him crying, asking him to let me go. The more I
asked him to let me go, the tighter he got, cutting off my
wind. He said, "This is my last time. Look me in my face
and tell me you don't want me." Not knowing what was
next, I knew I was dead so I said, "I don't want you."
Black still had me by my neck. He pushed in up against
the wall and said, "I hope he got AIDS or something."
He let me go. I stood there crying and holding my neck. I
told him to leave and don't come back. He walked off and
said, "You will pay. Believe that." He walked off as I

stood outside crying and trying to get myself together. I walked back in and Steve was on the side of the bed with his clothes on. He said, I'm getting ready to go. I don't do drama." He got up and left. I laid there in my bed crying, not knowing what to do. A day passed and Steve didn't call. I made up in my mind that he was gone and he wasn't coming back. I didn't call. I went to work. I got ready to get off when the front desk paged my beeper. I called the front desk. They needed me to come to the front lobby because someone was there to see me. I was like who is this now. I don't want to be brought with no one. I was done with men. I said I was going to be like my auntie and go out with a women. I went to the lobby. There was Steve standing there looking sexy. I said, "Hi." He said, "I don't get a hug?" I gave him a hug and on the inside I was saying, "Thank you God. You sent him back." He said, "I'm sorry for how I left the other night. I was upset, not with you, but with him. I didn't want you to see me like that." At that time he could have told me anything because I just wanted him in my life. He said, "Well, can I come over?" I said, "Sure, but I can't promise you that old boy want be back because he said if he can't have me, nobody can." He laughed and said, "I'm not worried about that." I said, "You sure? You left the other night and he could have come back and killed me" We laughed, "He said I will be here to pick you up". So the next morning he got up and got ready for work. I said, "Your keys are on the counter next to your house key." He looked and said, "What. I get a key." I said, "Yes, and I would love if you used it on a daily basis. I was off that day and had cooked. Steve came over and when he unlocked the door, I was standing there in the kitchen making his plate. I was so glad to see him walk through the door. He brought his clothes in and started putting them in the room. After he got set, we ate. We began making love again and again all night and all day. Life was good. I had it all, but not a baby. I didn't care at this point because I had a man in my life who was there with me, nice to me, and bought me what I wanted. I was good. On Sunday I got up and got dressed to go to church with one of my co-workers. I ask him if wanted to go. He didn't. He didn't mind if I went. I was only going because the girl kept asking me. I knew about church. I went to church with my grandmother; she was a usher I went with my dad; he was a deacon and I sing in the junior choir. So I knew about church, but I really didn't care if I went because I saw how my granny acted and how my dad partied. I said there was no need for me to go to church and still feel the way I did and things still happened to me. What was the point?. But I went because my co-worker asked me. When I came back from church and walked in my house, my house looked like someone had come in and redone it. There was a big TV with surround sound, a computer, a big glass dinner table and photos on it. He just knew I did not care, I didn't. I walked in and he was in the kitchen cooking Sunday dinner. He said, "Do you like it? Are you ok with having this stuff in here?" He had put a pole behind the glass door so Black could not get in. I was good. I had it all together. I was on a roll, doing me and living it up. We were going to work. He paid the rent. I paid the utilities. Everything was good until one day we got in to it. He went into the room, got his keys and some of his clothes and he got ready to leave. I said, "Before you leave give me back the key to my house." He walked out with some of his clothes and slammed the door. I feel to my knees crying. He came back in to get the rest of his clothes and give my key. I jumped up and went in the room crying and saying, "Wait, don't this. We can work through this. Don't leave." I could not be alone. I asked him not to leave. If I knew what was next, I would have just let him go on. So he hugged me and said, "I'm sorry." I said I was sorry too. We made up and had sex that night. Everything is good. Life was great. For Valentine's Day, he bought me a Jeep so I could get to and from work. My body started acting crazy. I was getting sick. I was throwing up and my period did not come. I didn't know what was going on. I thought my cancer was getting worse. One morning I got up and told Steve I needed to go to the doctor. I did not tell him I had cancer because I did not want him to leave me. I went to the doctor. Now, I had been drinking alcohol daily, having sex and doing whatever. Steve said, "I'm off today. Do you want me to go. I said no because I did not want him to know I had cancer. I told him I would be back and let him know what the doctor said. I went to the doctor and the lady was asking questions. She said, "When was your last period?" I told her it had been about a month and a half ago. She said, "Are you having sex?" I told her yes. She asked if I could be pregnant. I told her, "No, the doctor said I can't have kids because I have ovarian cancer." She asked, "When was the last time you've been to the doctor?" I said, "When I was fifteen or sixteen." She said, "You're not being treated?" I said, "No." She said, "Well, I need to take some blood." I told her ok but I was not with child. She came back and asked if I had been drinking a lot. I said, "Yes." She said, "I need you not to drink anymore until after you have your baby." I looked at that doctor and said, "Ma'am, you're lying. I can't have kids. You're lying. You must have gotten the wrong blood." She said no but she would check because there were four other ladies that had blood work done. As I sat there waiting, I was happy but scared at the same time. When she came back, she said it don't matter whose blood work I got back because all of us were with child. I cried as the doctor told me where I need to go so I could go to get help and get treated because my child was at risk. I returned home. I sat on the bed as Steve got ready to go to his mother house to let me met them. He asked, "Is everything ok?" I said, "Yes, but I have something to tell you." He said, "What" and looked at me crazy as if he wanted to curse. I said, "I'm pregnant." He said, "For real? How many months are you?" I said I didn't know until I went back to the doctor. He said, "You sure it's mine?" I said, "Wow. Who else's would it be?" At that moment I did not want to be pregnant. I didn't say anything else. He said, "You were still with your ex." I said I know, but the last few weeks I was not with him. I knew who and when I had sex. I was so mad and did not want to go meet his folks. But, I did. That whole week I did not say much to him. I didn't want him to leave, so I just did what he wanted me to. I tried not to make him mad, but everything I did made him mad. He would leave and stay gone all night not calling or anything. Little did I know, he was with some other woman having sex with her. I didn't want to work anymore. I hated working at the hospital, so I just up and quit without giving two week's notice or anything. I just walked off. The same week I got a job at the Marriot Hotel. It was ok because I went in at 9 am and got off at 3 pm. After being there for a month, I didn't like working there. I quit there and started working at Sears. I loved that job. I was selling clothes. I worked all kind of hours on that job. Steve didn't care because he was out doing him. Now the stealing demon was about to hit home. Me and my cousin Marta began talking again. I told her I was pregnant. She asked if the daddy was Black. I told her no, Black and I had been broken up for about two or three months. I told her what happened between me and Black that night he came to my house. I should have just kept my mouth closed. She said, "You sure Black is not the baby daddy?" I messed up and said that was the same thing Steve asked me. Marta was getting info from me to tell Steve. She would go his job and tell him he wasn't the baby's daddy and I was just playing for his money. She told him that I lied, stole, I was a (w****) and that I slept with anybody. She also told him I didn't graduate, I was dumb and all kinds of stuff She owed me some money and didn't pay it back to me, so I took her bank card and went to the ATM to get my money. That was my rent money I let her hold. Steve had stopped paying the bills. We would just yell and fight. He would slap me here and there sometimes. I was still going to work and she said I had stolen her card and took money off her card. I told him I didn't because I was doing me and he was doing him. I knew in my heart he was going to leave, I didn't know when, but I knew soon. Now Marta had started mess in my home. I was going to work stealing from Sears, getting gift cards and buying clothes for me and a baby bed and things for the baby. I was showing. Steve was not helping. And on top on that, I was riding with a another friend and taking her to the ATM. She gave me the bank card and the pin and I got money out for her because I thought it was her card. I came to find out, it wasn't. It didn't stop there, I stealing stuff for my granny, and my auntie's boys so she would forgive me for running away. She acted if she cared and as if she had forgiven me. She knew I was with child. She was happy and called my mother, but I didn't want to talk to my mother because I still hated her. I didn't have anything to say to her and she didn't have anything to say to me. I had lost my job and had a warrant out for me for petty theft and fraud. I was lying to Steve about going to work. I would get up and put on clothes like I was going to work because I didn't want him to know I was fired and was going to jail for stealing. Steve went to my job and found out I been fired because of stealing, so now he really isn't coming home. He was out and about with the new girl. I got a job really couldn't work because I was seven months pregnant and I was too big. My last day there I went home and when I got there I saw a big U-Haul truck leaving my house. Steve looked at me and didn't saying anything. I went in the house and Steve had taken everything out my house that he brought. All I had was my bed, because the couch I had I let go back to Aaron's Rental because he had gotten a couch from his job. I had nothing. Bill were due. Things were getting cut off. The Jeep was messing up. I was getting ready to be put out. I was seven months getting ready to be eight months and I couldn't stay with my granny because she didn't want me there. My auntie was in jail, so I couldn't go there. All, except one of my uncles were are locked up and my mom and I weren't talking. I don't know what to do. My back was against the wall. On the last day in my place, I packed all my stuff in the car. Now, I was living in the Jeep. I got my last check and went and stayed at this nasty motel. My uncle George's wife Barbara saw my car and she stopped. She said, "Your mom's here. I said, "That's good." She said, "What are you doing over here?" I said, "Staying." She said, "What happened to your house?" I said, "I got put out. I don't have a job. I'm too big." So she said, "Well, I'm on my way to your granny's house because she cooked and you're coming." I got dressed and we went down there. When I got there my granny said, "There goes my baby." My mother said,

"Who?" My granny said, "Kashia." My mother asked me what was I having. I told her a girl. She began to say things out of her mouth that were hurtful to me, so I asked my uncle's wife to back home. My uncle's wife said, "Victoria take Kashia home." She was trying to get my mother to see where I stayed thinking she would help me, but my mother said, "How did she get here? That's how she needs to get back." I got up and walked out as my uncle went off on my mother. His wife came outside and they asked me was I ready to go. We got in the car and my uncle began to talk about my mother. I cried as his wife told him what was going on. He said, "You can come stay with us until you have the baby." I told them ok. I went back to the room and stayed the night. As I laid there crying and looking for a way out, I wanted to get in my car and drive off a bridge somewhere. The next day I went and moved in with my uncle and his wife. As she laid down the rules, I was like oh my gosh I could have just stayed on the street. But she took me and got me on WIC, Food Stamps, Medicaid and A.F.D.C. I was good. Steve called me and said he needed the Jeep, so I told him to come and get it. I was on my feet when Steve started coming around and wanted to get back together. I didn't want anything to do with him. My aunt told me what I needed to put him on child support, so after he saw that it wasn't nothing between us, we stopped talking. I stayed there with my uncle and his wife and they began to have marital problems. Her people didn't know she was married to my uncle. They had hidden it from her folks. They would get in to it and she would tell my uncle that he and I needed to get out. One day I was in the room and I heard them talking about me. They said that I was sleeping too much and was not helping do anything.

Chapter 13

I'm about to lose my mind

I was back at granny's house. As we pulled up my uncle took my stuff out of his car and walked in my granny's house. She said, "What is this?" He said, "Kashia's coming to stay with you. She can't stay with me and my family. She has too much baggage. Granny said, "You should have called me before you brought her over here. I don't want her here neither." So he said, "Send her to her mother." She said, "Her mother don't want her neither." I stood there listening to them. I was so hurt and mad and looking for a place to go. The minutes on my phone had gone out, so I asked her if could I use her phone. She looked at me and said no there was a pay phone around the corner. I looked at her like I wanted to kill her. I got ready to walk out and she said, "Get your (s***) and put it up." I said, "Where do you want me to put it? You don't want me here." She got smart so I took my stuff and put it in the back room. I went outside and that when I met Vernon and Mrs. Mary Ann. Vernon said, "You are Kashia." I said, "How do you know me." She said, "I have heard so much about you. I see you all the time when you come over and bring your granny all them clothes." I said, "Hmm, so you know all about me." She laughed and said, "I do." I said, "That's no surprise. I'm the black sheep in the family." We laughed and said, "We will get along well," We were talking when Mrs. Mary Ann came outside. Mrs. Mary Ann said, "Girl, you better get from over here. Your granny don't like us and she don't want nobody from over there over here. She thinks we have something to do with the neighbor watch and getting on the news." I looked at them and said, "Baby, that house was getting kicked in when I was a baby. Don't worry about that." We continued talking and they asked when was the baby due. I told them October 30, a few weeks away. So as we talked Mrs. Mary Ann's son, Eric, pulled up, Eric looked at me and said, "Hi." I said, "Hi." He said, "Somebody knocked you up good." I laughed and he introduced himself. I told him my name. I looked at him and said to myself, take me with you. His sister and mother said, "This is Mrs. Godwin's granddaughter. He started laughing. We talked for a minute. He made sexual comments; I made them back. His mother and sister laughed and said, "We are not responsible for what happens." I said, "Well, he's grown and I'm grown, How old are you?" He said, "Forty-two." I thought, a sugar daddy. I used to hear my mother say sugar daddy when she was dating men older then her. He said, "How old are you?" I said, "Do you really want to know?" He said, "Yes. Eighteen?" I said, "No, twenty and I getting ready to turn twenty-one in January." He said, "January what?" I said, "The eighth." He said, "I'm on the fifteenth." We laughed as his mother said, "I see my next daughter-in-law." Eric looked up and said, "You're right." Eric had to go back to work so I told him I would talk to him later. I got ready to walk to the store when he said he would take me. We were talking about my folks. He said, "I know them Godwin's." I said, "I don't need to say any more". We went in the store and he bought me something to eat. I went to buy minutes. He said, "I got it." I said, "No, I'm good." He said, "No, I do. I got you." I looked at him and said to myself, "This going to be my sugar daddy. I will give him some and get what I need for me and my baby." When I got back home my granny said, "You knock before you walk in my house." I said, "Ok." Then she said, "I saw you talking to (m**f*****) over there. I don't want them over here and you're not going to be going over there staying in my house." I didn't say nothing. So weeks went by and I'm due at any time. My cousin Marta came over my granny's house and looked at me and spoke. I didn't say anything to her because she was the reason why I didn't have my man anymore. I went and got in the bed. She left and within about forty-five minutes the police came to my granny's house and asked if I was there. She said, "Yes." She came in the back and said, "Kashia, get up the police are here and have a warrant for your arrest." When I got up they asked me my name, looked at me and said, "When are you due." I said, "On the thirtieth." He said, "That's in a few days. I can't believe a person would call and turn you in three days before it's time for you have your baby." They got ready to take me to jail and I said, "Would you get my purse because my money is in there and I have money to bond out." When we got out to the car he said, "I can't tell you who called in" and he began to read my charges. I told him I knew my cousin Marta because she had just left about forty-five minutes ago. He said, "Well, I don't have to say any more." So I got to the jail and they booked me. I was mad and upset because I didn't want my baby to be born in jail. I was so mad at Marta. I sat there thinking of ways to get her. So I didn't call my granny's because I knew she didn't care and she wasn't coming to get me. So the lady at the jail said, "You will have to stay the night and see the judge in the morning." They took me to the infirmary because I was so close to my due date. There were two other ladies in that room and I could tell that they had been there more than once because when they asked me what my charges were they told me to plead no contest. They said since this was my first time they were going to put all my charges together.

If I pled no contest and told them I was getting ready to have my and that I was going to college, I would be ok. They also said I should beat my cousin for doing that mess so close to having my baby. I sat there crying while they talked to me like a mother and told me what to do. The next morning I did and said everything the ladies told me. The judge let me go, but I was on house supervision for six weeks. I had to report every day to my parole officer, Mr. David. I had two years on probation, twenty-five hours of community service, and I had to pay fines, one for $174 and another for $2000. I was good because I got money from A. F. D.C. I called my granny to come get me and when she answered the phone she said, "I don't have any money to come get you, so I don't know what you're going to do." I told her they let me go, I just needed a ride. When she picked me up, she acted like she was so mad at Marta and kept saying what she was going to do to Marta when she saw her. But she wasn't really going to do anything. She dropped me off back home and left me there to watch my auntie's kids while she went to bingo I just went outside and sat on the porch. My uncle came to the house and said, "You one of use now. You've been to jail like all of us," I didn't say nothing because I was mad about how they treated me, I didn't want anything to do with them. My Uncle Mike came to the house talking mess, I just looked at him because I hated him too. I didn't want him talking to me so I went next door to talk to Vernon and her mother. I went and checked in every day like I was supposed to and they told me after I had my baby that I could start doing my community service hours. They told me to check in every day up until I got ready to have the baby and once I went in to call so my parole officer could come and check on me while I was in the hospital. So things were good,

October 30 came, but no baby. The weekend was here and we were messing with my granny and saying my baby was going to come while she was at bingo. Granny said, "Have it and when I get there, I get there." I was hurt. My mom called and asked me what I had for the baby. I told her and she said she was sending me a box that should be here that day. I thanked her and I asked if she was off that weekend. She said, "Yes, but I won't be there because I don't have any money to go up there. I will see your baby when I come up there in a few months. I was mad, but I just said ok. As she and my grandmother were talking, my granny said, "I won't be there either, I will be at bingo if she has the baby this weekend," On November 3 I didn't say anything to my family. I stayed to myself and talking to Vernon and her mother as she laughed and said I needed to have the baby. Vernon told me to go walking. So I did. I walked to Wing To Go on 9th Avenue and got something to eat. When I came back my cousin Benson, some of his friends and Larry were there. I sat on the floor eating and as I sat there I began having labor pains. My cousin asked me what was wrong. I said I think I'm going in labor. He asked if I wanted to go to the hospital. I said no not right now and sat there for about two hours. The pain got worse and I started crying. My cousin said, Come on. Where's your stuff?" As he and his boys stood by my side he asked me if I wanted him to call Steve. I said yes so he called and told him I was in labor and Steve said he would be up there when he could. When my cousin told me what he said, I knew he was not coming. I didn't worry about it. I wanted to call Eric, but we were just friends we had not even been on a date. So I didn't say anything. Things were getting worse. I wanted to have my baby natural, but because the baby was in distress, the nurses had to give me an epidural. They came back in about an hour to check me. I laid there crying because I wanted Steve and he wasn't there. I wanted my mother; she wasn't there. I wanted my granny; she wasn't there. The only people that were there in my room with me were my cousin Benson and his boys. As they wiped my face and head and held my hand, I was mad in stress and depressed. I just wanted my baby to get here because I knew then I would have someone to love me and I would love her like my mother did not do me. So the doctor came in and she said she had to do a C –Section. I said ok as she explained what a C-Section was. I said ok and signed the consent form. She said only one person could go back there and asked if the dad was here. I said no and asked Benson to call him again. He did, but when he called Steve, Steve had turned his phone off. Everybody was mad at Steve and all Benson's friends wanted to fight him. She asked if I wanted someone to come back with me. I said my cousin because I was scared and even though he did what he did, I needed him at that time. So here it is. My baby girl is here looked just like me when I was a baby—fat, light skin with brown freckles on her face and a head full of hair, They wrapped her up and brought her to me so could see her. I cried because I had joy. I had my own child, someone that loved me and I loved her. So that next day, my granny came to the hospital and said, "Ok, you alright? I'm going to see my great grand." She had to wait in the room until the nurse came to put her band on so she could go see the baby. The baby was in a glass case. The nurses had to watch her and give her medicine. because she'd had a bowel movement and swallowed some of it. She was also a breach baby. My granny stayed back there with my baby for about hour, When she got done she stopped back by the room and said, "I'm gone. I came out and saw who I wanted to see." When she closed the door I said, "Don't get happy because you won't have her." I stayed in the hospital for a week. When we go better, I called Steve and asked him if was he coming to see his baby. He said, "No, because I don't know if that's my baby or not." I hung up in his face crying and mad, The more I sat there, the more I thought of all that voodoo stuff I used to do. I was going to get him and my cousin Marta. Now I wanted them die. The nurse had me filling out papers when she asked, "What did you name her?" I said, "Marie King." She said, "That's nice. And you didn't give her anything she can't spell when she gets in school." I laughed. So me and my baby went home that Sunday night about 11:00. My granny came and got us. It was cold. I was cold. I was back down to a size 9/10. We got home. I had milk from the hospital that lasted for about a month so I didn't have to make any bottles. Things were good. I didn't want anyone to hold her or kiss her. I had to report to house supervision. My P. O. told me I could do my hours in February since I just had the baby. I was at home with my baby. She was a week old. I was in the house, the only places I went was to the check in with my P. O., to the doctor and back at home. I took my child everywhere I went. Thanksgiving came and we had to go out to My uncle George house. He was the one who told me I couldn't stay with him and his family. I didn't want to go but my granny said don't act like that. So I went and when I got there I started acting real crazy. I didn't eat anything and my uncle's wife noticed. My uncle said, "The hell with you. You shouldn't have come, you or your (b*****) child. I looked at him, got my baby and said, "Granny, I'm going to get in your car and that's where me and my child will be." I looked at him and his wife and said, "At least I have a child and I don't have to married to no one that can't tell their family we're married. You don't have to worry about me and my child coming back to your house. You will need me before I need you." I walked out and went and got in the car. My granny came out and acted like she was mad at my uncle. I just looked at her because they were just on the phone talking weeks ago. Eric was over his mother's house and when I got out he said, "Can I see the baby?" I went over there; I didn't care what my granny said. I had my baby and the doctor told me I was good. He said I didn't see any cancer. I went back down to size and I didn't a warrant out on me. It was time for me to start using what I had to get what I needed for me and my child. I was ready to get out that hell hole. I sat over there with Eric and his mother and ate with them. I got myself something to drink when Eric's mother said, "You're not breastfeeding her?" I said, "No ma'am, that hurts." I stayed over there just about all day and let them play with the baby. Me and Eric began talking and making plans to go out. I said, "When my baby gets a few months, I will see." He said, "No, you can bring your baby, I mean our baby." I said, "What?" He said, "Her daddy isn't going to step up. I will be her daddy." And he did just that, He began buying for her, giving me money, paying my probation stuff, buying me food, and taking me where I needed to go, Every day he would come over his mother's house so we got closer. He had a woman that he stayed with and a woman he had just broken up with, but I didn't care because I said I wasn't giving my heart to anyone else. It was all about the money and what I could get from him. So every day I would get up and get me and my child ready and about noon we went over Eric's mother's house. She stayed next door, so I was over there every day. I gave my granny the money that I got from the state because she said her bills were going up since I was there. I was not there like that because I would stay gone all day until about six and I wasn't eating at her house. All I did was go to bed and take a bath. She would get mad because I didn't need her for anything. Big Joe would come by. I didn't like him at all. She would tell him and my mother that I didn't let her keep my baby and that I would get up and leave and didn't see if she needed anything. I did because she didn't want me there. I would leave so I didn't have to listen to her. Knowing what she had to say, I went and applied for a job working at Bally's Grocery Store. When I went to work I would let Eric's mother keep the baby. So one day I was off and I had to go check in. I was over Eric's mother's house and my uncle Mike came over and started going off on me and hitting me. I went in the kitchen to get a knife. My granny said, "Let her cut you so she will go to jail and her baby will be in foster care like she was." I came out the kitchen and told him, "If you put your hands on me again this time you will go to jail." I called him a child molester. My granny said, "What did you say?" I said, " I said your son touches little kids." His girlfriend was there and they all said I was lying. My grandmother called me all kind of names. I said, "I'll be whatever you call me but I know what is and what isn't. This isn't what I heard, this is what I know. I went back over to Eric's mother's house to get ready to go check in. My uncle Mike came over and said, "You stay over here more than you do at my mother house. Eric, you're with her, find her somewhere to stay." So he put me out of my granny's house. While Eric was at his mother's house, I went and got me and my baby's stuff and took it to Eric's mother's house because she said I could stay there. She was not going to put me and the baby out on the street. I told her I would give her the money I was giving my

Granny for letting us stay. She said, "No, Eric has it and you already give me money for keeping your baby." I went go to go and check in with my parole officer and let him know I moved next door so I wouldn't get in trouble. Mike came back over to Mrs. Mary Anne's and told them they had better watch me because I steal and lie and was no good. When I got back they told me what he said so I told them he was mad because his mother and his girlfriend just found out why I really hated him So they looked at me like and asked why I hated him so much. I told them and Eric's mother said she knew it was something about him that was not right. Months and months went on, I went to work, and checked in. Eric and I would go to the motel and have sex or we would have sex at his mother's house. Eric lived and went home to his baby's mama. I didn't care because it was all about me and mine and he was doing what I needed him to do. I was getting ready to get on HUD.I was going to the classes and doing everything they told me to do. I had to go and get a background check. I had done my community service hours and was paying on my probation. But, I forgot about the fine for $ 174. When I went and to the jail to do my background check, the police called me in the back and told me there was a warrant for my arrest. I told them there wasn't because I had already been to jail and hadn't done anything else. The officer said, "You have a fine for $174 you didn't pay and you don't have a bond. It said 30 days in jail." I went crazy because I going to jail and I would have to stay there for 30 days. I didn't want my baby over my granny's house and the HUD housing was going to give my place to someone else. I said, "Sir, I have the money. Can I just go ahead and pay it?" He said, "No, because you were supposed to have paid that in two months." They let me talk to Eric and I told him not to let anyone get my baby and to let my baby stay with his mother. Eric said ok. He wrote the judge, he went and talked to the judge. But they would not let me out. The whole weekend I was stuck like Chuck, mad and worried about my baby. When my granny got the paper and saw I was in jail, she tried to go get my baby. Eric's mother told her she couldn't give her the baby because I said no one gets the baby unless it's the daddy (and she knew the daddy because she got a couch from his store). While I was in jail, Eric sent money and wrote. He wanted to come see me and bring the baby to see me, but I told him no because I didn't want him or my baby to see me like that. Time went on and I got out. Granny had my baby because she was acting crazy and said she was going to call the police. Eric's mom let my granny have my baby. When she went to bingo, she took my baby back over to Mrs. Mary Ann house. I was mad. When I got out, Eric was there waiting on me. We went to the hotel and had sex all night, My demon was weak and I needed to feed it. I was also hungry because I did not eat the stuff they feed us in jail. I was so hungry I went to Wendy's and to our spot downtown. I asked him who had my baby and why didn't he bring her. He said, "Your granny has her and she's been real nasty to us about her. I told mama let her go because we did not want Marie in foster care." I said ok and I would handle it in the morning. The next morning I went back to Eric's mother's house and I said, "Where is she?" She told me the same thing Eric told me. I went next door and my granny said, "I knew you were getting out. That's why they wanted your baby, but I told him, I was the grandmother." I looked at her and I said she was doing what I told her. No one was get my baby, not even my mother. I looked at my baby and I held her and hugged her as she smiled. I was mad at my granny. She said, "Do you have a place to stay?" I said, "Yes, I'm going back where I was." I got my baby and went back to Mary Ann's house. I was so mad, I was cursing and going off. Mary Ann said, "What's wrong?" I said, "Look at my baby. She's dirty. She smell's nasty and her hair is not done." Vernon, her mother and Eric all knew I was going to cut up because she I didn't play about my child. My baby was always dressed and looked good. I went and checked in and they told me I wasn't in trouble. It was an honest mistake and I could do the rest of my time on house supervision. So time went on and I would talk to my grandmother but not like that because they were trying to start mess between me and Eric's mother so she would put me out. Eric was with me. The woman he had broken up with started coming around. My granny found out who she was and told her about me. The woman wanted to fight me, but every time it got down to it, Eric would not let me fight her because he knew I would go to jail for two years. Granny has started mess with me, Eric's mother and sister. I came back from checking in with my P.O. Granny, my auntie's kids, Mary Ann, Vernon and her nieces and nephews are all outside. I looked at Eric and said, "What's going on now?" I got out of the car and my grandmother went to cussing me out. I said, "I don't have time for this." Mary Ann said, "No, come back out here. We're going to talk about this because your granny said you've been saying things about us." I listened to what she had to say and I called my granny a lie to her face. By this time the lady across the street came outside to watch. We were going back and forth. Granny called me a (B****). I called her one back. She came up on the porch and slapped me. I went to hit her back and Eric jumped in front of us to keep me from hitting her. My cousin ran around the corner to go get my cousin Benson. Then he got up in my face and got ready to hit me. I said, "Oh, you're going hit me?" He cursed me out and told me he hated me. In the end, Eric's mother said, "Kashia, you hit your grandmother. I can't have staying here." And she put me out of her house.

Chapter 14

Ready to Receive

Well here I am moving in with Alyssa and her kids and her boyfriend Eric's baby sister. As I was on my way there, my grandmother and Eric's mother call Alyssa and try to tell her all this stuff about me and try to make me look bad so Alyssa would not let me and my child stay with her. But Alyssa said I'm not going to let that girl stay on the street and I not going to let her go to jail and she just had a baby. So as Ms. Godwin and Mrs. Mary Ann got mad at Alyssa and decided that they would start trouble for her house by calling HRS on me and saying I'm at unfit mother so HRS could come out to Alyssa's house, and calling HUD to tell that Alyssa had other people staying in her house that were not supposed to be there. But everything they tried did not work. So they called Eric's ex-girlfriend and told her that Eric and I were together and he had moved out to his sister's house. So the young lady Dana came out to Alyssa house to fight me but Alyssa made me go in the house because she didn't want me to go back to jail and she didn't want the police to come to her house because I was not supposed to be there in her house,. Alyssa called Eric at work and told him that he was going to have to find me a place soon because she could not have that heat at her house. After Mrs. Mary Ann found out that what they were doing was hurting Alyssa and not Kashia, Mrs. Mary Ann stopped. But Ms. Godwin did not stop until she tried everything she could. So the next morning I went to the court house and filed a restraining order against my granny and my uncle Mike and his son Benson and told everything I knew about them from the drugs to the guns to the dog that Benson killed and buried in the back yard. I was mad and I was out to make their life a living hell. Every devilish demon that was in me was used that day to hurt my family. I called my mother and she acted as if she did not care. I told her what happened and that I could be going to jail because of this mess. She said that's on you but if you do go to jail I will be there to get my grandchild. I got madder and hung up the phone with her saying to myself this is some bull how is my mother going to say that is on me but she will be here to get my baby if I go to jail. I went off as Eric looked at me and said if we go and have some papers drawn up for me to get Marie, no one can get her. So we went to a place to have the papers draw up so no one could get my child but Eric. So the more Eric did for me, the more my love changed. It became more than just sex and what he could do for me. He said he loved me and this time it was more than someone just saying he loved me, he also showed me. I was beginning to fall in love with him. I didn't care about the other woman because we would talk and he would tell me how she was not doing this and not doing that. So as weeks went on my granny, uncle and my cousin got served their papers by the police and we all had to go to court. As we waited for the court date, my family began to tell Mrs. Mary Ann what they were going to do to me and Eric. Mrs. Mary Ann got worried and called Alyssa to tell her so Alyssa would tell me. But I did not care because I felt safe knowing I was with Eric and he was smart. He knew what I had to do and he knew what they could not do. So that day of court I asked Alyssa if would she keep Marie and she said yes. She would tell me all the time leave the baby with her and her kids, and that Marie would be safe because she knew how I was with Marie. But because of what had happened to me I could not trust anyone with my baby which is why I had to do everything in my power to stay out of jail. I did not want any of my family to get my baby and I did not want my baby to in up in foster care. But Alyssa said yes she could stay and I told her if anything happened to keep my baby until Eric got off work. She smiled and said you will be ok. Then Eric said you not going to jail, if anything they will be going to jail because they like to act up and the courts are not going for that. So as we leave and get to the court house we get there and we are sitting there and as we sit there waiting on court, Ms. Godwin, Mike, Benson and Mike's girlfriend walked in and looked at me as if they wanted to kill me. As our names were called to see the judge, we walked up and the judge began to ask questions about the case and why I filed the order against my family. As I began to talk, Mike got loud and tried to talk over me. The judge looked at him and told him that he would get a turn to speak. As I gave my side, the judge turned to my grandmother who began to tell the judge how I went to jail for stealing, how I'm a unfit mother, and how I lie and that Eric is too old for me and how Eric uses his company car to take me places while he at work. The judge looked her and said Ms. Godwin we are not here for all that I don't care about what she went to jail for I don't care who she is dating I just want to know why are you all bothering her and this man. So Ms. Godwin got quiet and didn't have anything to say. So the judge went to Benson and asked him what do you have to about this. Benson replied and said nothing, I do not know why I'm even here. The judge looked and said did you or did you not go over to where Ms. King was staying and jump up in her face telling her you will beat her you don't care about Eric standing there, Benson said yes so the judge looked at Benson and said ok that's why you are here, so

Benson just stood there looking at the judge. As the judge turned and looked at Mike and said ok what do you have to say Mr. Godwin. As Mike began to talk he started talking about how I went to jail and how I'm with a man that is 20 years older than me and how I'm moving from house to house with an infant. As the judge looked at Mike and said I just told your mother we are not here for all that. And the judge looked back at me and asked me what do I want. As I looked at the judge and said I just want them to leave me alone. I want them to stay out my life and not say nothing to me or my child and quit calling the people where I stay telling them what they are going to do to me. As the judge looked at Eric and said how old are you. Eric said I'm 42. And then he looked at me and asked how old are you. As I looked at him and said 21. The judge looked at my family and said she is old enough to date who she want. I can't see why you all are giving her a hard time. So I will order you all to stay 500 feet away from Ms. King. As Eric and I walked outside, we could hear them saying this is not over. And not over is just what they meant. So as weeks went on I thought everything was fine. I was getting my life back. There was no more drama and no more Godwin. It was just me, my child and Eric. Not. So here it is. I went to check in with my probation officer. As I tell her what's going on she says I know Mr. David has already told me and if anything happens I will make sure you don't go down the road. So back at my granny house, my granny and my uncle and Eric's mother and Vernon were sitting at Mrs. Mary Ann house with a video camera making a video saying I hit my grandmother and I messed up her face and she had to go to the hospital because I had hurt her. They went to the jail house to press charges on me. Now I'm on probation and had just got off of house supervision when I get the hit with a new charge. So as I get picked up for that and have to pay a bond of $250. I'm looking at going back to jail, at least that's what Mrs. Godwin and her son thinks. As I called Eric to let him know what is going on he comes to bail me out. As I go back to my probation officer, she tells me don't worry about it you have already told me what is what so I will have your probation reinstated. So I was happy, but I was mad because they would not just leave me alone. As I sit there mad but thanking God because I know it was His grace and mercy that I didn't go down the road for one. So as I go and see my public defender, he asked me was I guilty or not and I said not guilty. He began to tell me what could happen because I said I'm not guilty. He said that it would be a trial and if I was found guilty I would go to jail for two years. I began crying and right there I began asking God to please get me out of this mess. Once again God showed up and because of his grace I was not found guilty. Mrs. Mary Ann and Vernon did not go to court and lie for Mrs. Godwin. I had a witness that was ready to tell the truth about the whole thing that happened on that day. So after all of that and nothing was working in their favor they gave up trying to get me locked up. So I had made up in my mind that I was going to get myself together and get me and my baby our own place and leave my family alone and be with Eric and get in church. So as everything died down, I was still at Alyssa's. I was not talking to my family and I was not talking to Mrs. Mary Ann or Vernon. I still hated them; I did not like them and I did not care if I had ever seen them again. So here I am at peace. I have one more week on probation. Eric just took me to pay my last $110 dollars on my probation. I'm good and thanking God because he did it for me. All the hell I was going through is over, at least for a season. So here is Eric's one day off of work, he came to Alyssa's house and hugged me and kissed me on my head and said I would you like to go and see your place. I looked at him and said stop lying. He said no am for real. I began jumping up and down saying come on lets go. As we left, his sister asked oh you getting ready to move out. Eric said yes I found Kashia her own place it is time for her to get her own. As Alyssa looked in a way she was glad because with four grown women in the house it's going to be a little drama, but on the other she was sad because she was going to miss the money that she was getting from Eric for letting me and Marie stay with her. But as we went to the apartment, he opened the door and said this is it. He said well you can move in as soon as they turn the water and the lights on. I looked at Eric and said I can move in today, I went months without lights so what is two days. He began to laugh and said no you have a baby, my baby, and you all will not be in the dark or without water. So I said ok as I smiled because now he had stood up for me with my family. He is buying me and my baby any and everything we want. Now he has put me in my own place and on top of it all he said my baby is his child. Now I know that this man really does love me. It's not an act. Now my love for him had gotten deeper and I could not see any wrong in him. Still, he had a woman and kids that he went home to every night. But I was so in love about the little things, I was blind to the big thing that he was still going home to his baby mama, Lynne. And I guess she felt the same way. Because she knew about me. Her kids used to come and get their hair done by me when I stayed at my grandmother's house. I believe he was telling her one thing and telling me another, but I didn't care because I was in love. I felt like he was my Lord because everything I needed or wanted, he was right there. (Wrong) it was God's grace. So here we are in the apartment as we play husband and wife but yet still he goes home to his baby mama. So it was at this time I met his friend Carrie. Carrie was a cab driver and a mother of four and she was in the church. So as I began hanging out with Carrie she would take me where I needed to go and she would talk to me about stuff. Carrie was like the mother I wish I could have had. And the more I hung out with her, the more I learned. Even though Carrie was in the church, she would tell you what you needed to know and the things you did not need to know. As time went on, me and Eric would go places. I would go to the club with Eric. I would have all the sex he wanted to have. I would go to all his shows. We would do all kinds of thing together. And the more we did, the more I would tell Carrie, and the more she would tell me in so many ways. So now here I am thinking I got something and someone who loves me for me but all along he is still sleeping with his ex-girlfriend Dana and paying her bills and going home to his baby mama. So now I get mad because I felt like Eric was in love with me because of the stuff we went through with my family and his family and because he had gotten me and my child what we want and what me need. Eric had also bought me a wedding set saying he wanted to marry me, he wanted to be a family and he was going to leave his baby mama because she was not there for him, she did not cook and she did not make love to him. And I believed him. He would come to the apartment in the morning before work, during work, and after work. He would stay with me and my child until two and three in the morning and go home. Lynne would call and ask him where he was, but he would lie and say band practice or he had to play. Yep, he was playing alright. So as time went on we began get into it. We would yell,

144

scream and fight. He would grab me and pin me against the wall. I would hit him and go into the kitchen and get a knife to try to cut him because as a child that's what I had seen my mother do to her ex-husband. My mind went back to those days so I would just do what I had seen. So Carrie would tell me what Eric was out in the street doing so I would get mad and fight with him about. The more we fought, the more I pulled back from him. As I got closer to Carrie, she would ask me to go to church with her and I would make up all the excuses in the world why I could not go. So she began to tell me about her pastor and her church. As she would tell me about her church, I would ask her about her pastor. The more questions I asked, the more she gave. Every time me and Eric got in to it I would tell her and she would began to minister to me about church and how I have a call on my life and I will preach his word one day. I would just look at Carrie and said not me the devil is a lair. I like to have sex too much. I like going to the club and drinking. So as Carrie would still tell me that I needed to get in church because God had something great for me, I was like ok I will go with you one day. But in the meanwhile, who is this brother that's on this photo on your table. Carrie replied by saying that's my brother Willie. I said where does he stay. Carrie said in Texas. So I was like you need to hook me up. Eric is out doing his thing and it's time for me to do my thing and start seeing other people so if he decides to leave me like everyone else, I will have a plan B. So Carrie began laughing and saying well yes you are right about it. So now here I am with Eric at home. We just fight and yell with each other every day in front of our daughter and I said something has got to get better. As the week went on, I would call Carrie and tell her about my fights with Eric, and she would just minister to me about the Lord. So one day me and Carrie was on the phone and her Bishop, Bishop Snow walked in and asked her who was she talking to. And she said a friend of mine I'm trying to get her to come to church with me Bishop, she is going through a lot with her boyfriend. So Bishop Snow got on the phone and he began to talk to me and while he was talking to me, I was letting the devil use me because Carrie had already told me how he was and what he loved to do for the women of the church. So he ask me why I wouldn't come to church and I lied and said I didn't have anything to wear. He said I will buy you something to wear. Then I said my hair was not done and I don't have any money to get my hair done. So Bishop was like we have about two or three women in the church who can do your hair. So as we talked I was not feeling him at first because he was talking church and I was talking dollars. So I got off the phone with the Bishop and I told Carrie to call me back when her pastor left. So weeks went by and me and Eric got in a bad fight. I called Carrie and told her I'm tired of this. So she said my brother is coming home this weekend and I said that's cool. I told Carrie it's on I'm about to do me. Eric still talking to his ex and going home to his baby mama. So I got off the phone with Carrie and I called Eric and told him I needed some money because I had to go to my mother's house. I knew he would give the money to see my mother because one, I am not in town and he can really be with his ex and two, he was trying to get on my mother's good side because my mother did not like him. Eric came to the house and gave me $500 dollars to go out of town with. I went and bought all new clothes, got my hair and my nails done, and bought my daughter all new clothes only to go across town to stay the week with Carrie's brother Willie. So I went over Carrie house that morning as if I was going out of town, but I sat there waiting on Willie to get there at the house. So when he got there, this fine, short build, brown skin, pretty eyes, bald head man come walking through the door. He looked at his sister and said hey baby girl as she smiled and hugged her brother and said well she here is Ms. Kashia. I stood up with my brown skirt with the split up to my thing and my brown and red shirt with my breasts pushed up and my hair pulled up in chop sticks looking and smelling all good. Willie said (D***) this is the Ms. Kashia I have been talking to every day. I said well it is I. Willie looked at his sister Carrie and said hum baby girl you did a good job with this one. Carrie laughed and said yes I did, this is my girl, take care of her. So I let him met my baby that day and he fell in love with her. Now he knew my situation with Eric and he didn't care. And at that point, I did not care neither. So the weekend went on. We left and went to the hotel and that night we had sex. I was in love, at least that's what I told myself because I wanted love. Just because a man made love to me how I wanted and when I wanted, I was in love, or shall I say lust. As the weekend went on, I was enjoying myself. Eric called and I would answer and act as if I was with my mother but I was right there in town. So as time went on I began getting closer to Willie. Eric and I were still getting into fights. I didn't care anymore about him because I had someone new in my life doing for me . So one day I decided to go to Carrie's church, New Birth Holiness Church, with her. So when I get there I met the Bishop and his wife and he began to talk to me and said I don't see nothing wrong with your head or your clothes so what is the problem why you have not been coming to church with sister Carrie. When I looked at him he smiled and I looked at him as I said to myself what kind of pastor is he with gold all in his mouth. I said he is a undercover drug dealer or something. As I smiled and thought about how I was going to get in with him to get his money and have sex with him. I was a hurt girl looking for love from any man that could make love to me like Luke did. I could not have who I really wanted, so I would be with the ones I thought was that one. So as time went on Bishop would put the chair out every service so people would join and the first few times I would not go because I had on short dresses and I did not feel right. But I would wear the short clothes so the bishop would say something about my clothes and go and buy me clothes because he said on the phone he would buy me some clothes, so I was trying him. His wife, Lady Snow, would look at me as if she could see what I was about, but she didn't say anything. As time went on, I joined the church and I became an usher in the church. I was coming to church, doing what the pastor and his wife asked me to do, but I was still fighting with Eric and having sex with Willie every month when he came home. Willie was in the army and would come home on the 15th of every month and stay two weeks. I would spend the first week with him and the second week, I would go over his sister's house and hang out with him, his sister, and his kids. So now I was in the church but not of the church. Meaning I was there, but I was not taking in the word and living it. So time went on and the more I worked closely with the bishop, the more friendly we got. And that friendly turned into more than just my pastor and my friend. It started with taking me out to eat to every Sunday or every week putting money in my hand. Sometimes it would be $100 at a time. One thing led to another and we began having sex on a regular basis. Now, I'm sleeping with three men at one time—Eric, who is my main dude; Willie, my part-time lover; and Bishop Snow, my pay master. I was loving it. Bishop Snow was a bad man. He helped me, his wife, and some other saints get a job where he worked. I did not have a car, so he told his wife to give me her car to drive back and forth to work. As I drove her car, the other saints were trying to find out what was really going on between me and the Bishop because they had never seen one of the saints drive one of cars and I was one of the new saints. But they could not prove I was one of his women because I never acted like me and him had anything going on. After church I would leave. I would not be all in his wife face and I did not flirt with him until he came to my home. He would only come when Eric was out of town with his band. But at this time, I was wild and out there. I did not care. The only person I cared about was my child, and she was too young to really know what was going on. She knew Eric was daddy; Willie was my best friend, and Bishop was our pastor. She knew Steve was her real dad, but she did not do him because he was not around as much. So through all of this, I find out I'm pregnant. I was like ok I'm not going to trip because I know who I slept with. So through all of this, I tell Willie and he told me he could not have kids because he had himself fixed. I believe him because his baby mama /wife was coming around to see who the light skin girl Willie kept coming home every month to see. She would say crazy stuff out her month while I would be over Carrie house. We had some little words, but nothing big because she would not fight me. She was about talk and I was about fighting. Carrie would not let me fight her and on top on that I did not want Eric to find out I was messing with someone else. So I told Bishop Snow. He was like ok whatever you need let me know. I'm used to this, if it is my baby, it's my baby. So I told him I was sleeping with

Willie, Carrie's brother and that I still with Eric and he was like ok that's cool. So I told Eric and he was so happy he began telling everybody in his family. I was sitting there praying it was Eric's because I knew he was a good father and I thought if this is his baby he would leave his baby mama and we would get married for real and be a family. And things were good at first. We yelled at each other but he didn't hit me while I was pregnant. But the ex-girlfriend Dana began to come around and began drama with me and Lynne. I was like whatever. So Eric and his baby mama got in to it bad and she packed up and left Mobile and moved back to Virginia. So now he was upset and mad because Lynne has left to go back home with her mother. So as Eric comes back to the house crying and mad and telling me about Lynne left with his kids, I looked at him like I didn't care because one, the ex was still in the picture and he was crying because this woman that he said that don't do nothing for him and she let the bills get cut off

was leaving. So I did not care. I called Carrie to come get me so I could be with her brother Willie. So I left to go be with Willie for the weekend. So here I am three months pregnant and I am at home. I had just got off work and Eric was in the house cooking. He went outside to throw out the trash and his ex-girlfriend was outside and wanted to talk to me. He came back in the house and said Dana is outside and she wants to talk to you. So I opened my door because I thought he was playing, but she was standing out there with two of her kids. So I said hold on and I went in my room and pulled out my pony tail. I went in the kitchen and got a knife and put it in my pants because I was ready for anything and the new law was if someone came to your house to hurt you, you have the right to hurt them. I was ready to kill. So as I walked out my house, she said Kashia I'm not here to fight you, but you need to know about Eric. She began to tell me some stuff he did and said. I knew she was not lying because she was saying things no one knew but me and him. So as Dana and Eric get into it, I looked at both of them and my child was standing there looking at all this. So I asked her what is this I here when you see me you was going to do this and do that to me and you was going to hurt my child. She said I did not say that. So I looked at Eric and said that is not what you told me. So she began to tell me what happened. How he came to her house with my child and they started to fight. I looked at both of them and said I don't care what you all do but if my child gets hurt I will kill both of you and your kids. She looked at me and I said you all doing all this here, did he tell you I'm three months pregnant with his child? Dana began to get mad and started cussing Eric out as I stood there laughing at the both of them. I turned and looked at Eric and said is that were you want to be. He said no. So I looked at her and told her don't come back to my house, don't come on my job and don't come around my child because the next time it won't be to talk. I walked off as she said I will get you Eric,. I looked at Eric; I was mad and hurt in the inside but I did not say anything to him for about a week. He would come home and come in the room with me and I would not say anything. I would not let him touch me and I did not want him to buy me anything. He did not know what to do. He would call Carrie so she would talk to me, but I did not want to hear it. So I began to get wilder. I would go to work and come home, get dressed and leave. I stopped cooking. I stopped having sex with him. I turned to the Bishop because at the time I was going though that with Eric, Bishop Snow's wife had left him. He needed someone and I needed someone. But I wanted him to get back at Eric. This time I did what I did because I wanted Eric to find out because of what he had done and he was still with Dana when my heart was really into him. I did not care what would happen next. I had been though a lot, what more could happen? So months and months went by when I met this girl named Nicey and her mother Minister Toler they had begun going to Bishop Snow's church again. We. got close and became best of friends talking every day on the phone We were being messy and doing some of everything and on top of that me and Mrs. Mary Ann and Vernon had started back talking and getting along. I would talk to them but not like before because I was still kind of upset about how they treated me. Me and my mom talked but not like we should because she still being nasty in her own little way. I just talked to her every four or five days so I wouldn't get mad at her and want to keep my child from her. So as I talked to my mother I didn't tell her what was going on. I just told her of the guys I was dating and that I was getting ready to have another baby. So she began to buy things for the new baby, so we were good, but not great. We never told each other we were sorry. We would just buy things for each other and that was our way of saying I'm sorry. On the last weekend before it's time for me to have my baby, Willie was home from Texas and wanted to be there for the birth of my baby. But I told him that would not be good and that if he couldn't have any more kids there was no reason why he should be there. I looked at him in his face and I told him we can't do this anymore. He was still married and his wife kept on with crazy junk and I wasn't trying to go back to jail. I told him I would always love him, but I had got to let him go. As I took him back to his sister's house, I sat there with tears

because I did not want to let him go. But for my good I
had to. We became friends and every time I saw him we
would make love with our eyes to each other and we
would hug each other and go our separate ways. That
Sunday in church Bishop Snow told everyone I was going
in the next morning to have my baby. To me it was so
funny because still no one knew anything about me and
Bishop. The Bishop threw a big baby shower for me and
bought all the food and cake all kind of gifts for my baby.
So I laughed because after church I told him I wanted him
at the hospital because I did not know if it was his baby or
Eric's baby. He said ok I will know when you have her if
it is mine or not. He said if it's mine I will give you a
thumb down if it's not mine I will give you a thumb up. I
laughed and when I got there he was there. Eric looked
like what is he doing here, so I said hey Bishop are you
ready to pray before I have the baby. He said yes. We
played it off and after he got done praying he went in the
waiting room. As I sat there waiting to have my baby, I
got a phone call from Alice, Willie's wife. She wanted to
know if she could come and be in the delivery room with
me while I had the baby. I said yes because I knew it was
not Willie's baby and she worked there so I said sure. I
knew that was the only reason for her to come because
she wanted to see if the baby was Willie's. I had a baby
girl. She was real light skin with a head full of hair and
twelve fingers. So when they got her cleaned up and they
brought her to me, I looked at her and her fingers and I
knew she belonged to Eric because his kids were born
with twelve fingers. I looked at her face and I saw that lip
and I knew for sure that she was Eric baby. I was at easy
and I was ready to fix my family. I was not going to be
with Willie; I was not going to be with Bishop Snow. I
was just going to be with Eric. The nurse looked at me

and asked what her name was. Eric looked at the baby and said Alexis. The nurse took Alexis to the nursery. Bishop Snow, Eric, another pastor, and Minister Toler were all in the room taking photos with Alexis and Bishop said tell Sister King thumbs up. Eric not knowing came back in the room and said Bishop said thumbs up. I began to laugh and thank God because now I was getting my house together and now I'm getting ready to get in church for real.

Now here I am. I just had the baby and I'm ready to get back to church because I'm ready to start over and put the past behind me and Eric. So things are good. Marie, Alexis, Eric and I are a family. I'm going to church, getting in the word and talking more to Minister Toler and her daughter, Nicey about church. I'm going over their house talking to them about church and things that were going on in my life with Eric. So now I'm in church for real and Eric then began to think I was with the Bishop. Now that started mess because he didn't want me going to church. We are sleeping in different rooms. Eric was still playing at the clubs, but he was staying out all times of the night. He was also lying to me saying he had to play at the club. All the stuff he was saying to me were the same things he use to tell Lynne, so I knew he was lying. But I did not care because my mind was on getting right with Jesus. So one day Eric came home and he was saying I was sleeping with the Bishop. I was tired of fighting with him and I knew what to say to get him mad, and that's what I did. I said yep I slept with Bishop and I was with Carrie's brother too. At first Eric thought I was just saying something to get him mad, but I was telling him the truth. Carrie, Carrie's cousin, and Alice had already told him which was why we would get into it. But they waited too late to tell him. By the time they did tell him, I was not messing with those guys any more, but I told Eric I was with them. I was in the kitchen getting ready to cook some chicken and the grease was warm and when I told him that Eric pushed the grease off the stove. The grease hit the wall and flew back on my leg. My babies were in the kitchen so I ran to jump in front of them because I did not know how hot the grease was. So when that happened I pulled out a knife and I cut him on his arm. It was a small cut, but because of the way he was bleeding I thought I had really hurt him. I went to church the next night and the pastor began to preach.

Everything he preached about fit me and what I was going though and what I had been though. The pastor began the altar call and he began singing, "Falling in Love with Jesus." I sat there crying and rocking and thinking about all the men I had been with and how I was in love with alcohol, pills, and sex. I said God I'm sick and I'm tired and I can't take any more. I need your help. I can't do this by myself. As I got to the altar I began to cry out more God help me, God help me, and I began to tell God about all demon spirits that lay in me. The pastor prayed for me and I felt the presence of God. After the pastor stop praying he said I going to have prayer every day at noon at the church and Evangelist Saldana will be over this prayer and it started tomorrow. So I began coming to prayer and I began calling on the Lord every day. Evangelist Saldana worked with me about an hour in a half whipping the demon spirits. For about a month, I was going to prayer. I was also working two jobs and taking care of my kids. Eric and I were still living together, but it was not nothing because I had cut off sex with him. I stopped cooking and I stopped playing house. He was in one room and I was in the other room. We would still fight because if I told him no when he wanted sex, he would take it. But the more I went to church, the more I was getting to where God wanted me to be. One day I went to prayer and I made up in my mind that today was the day I was not going to leave the altar until I got the holy ghost. I laid there at the altar crying, tarrying for the Lord and calling on Jesus. And that last time I called Jesus, I received the gift on the holy ghost. I was speaking in tongues, shouting and praising God like never before. I was now a new creature in Christ.

(TO BE CONTINUED)

Made in the USA
Las Vegas, NV
16 April 2022